JOURNAL OF THE HESSE-CASSEL JAEGER CORPS

AND
HANS KONZE'S
LIST OF JAEGER OFFICERS

Translated by
Bruce E. Burgoyne
Edited by
Dr. Marie E. Burgoyne and Bruce E. Burgoyne

HERITAGE BOOKS
2008

HERITAGE BOOKS
AN IMPRINT OF HERITAGE BOOKS, INC.

Books, CDs, and more—Worldwide

For our listing of thousands of titles see our website
at
www.HeritageBooks.com

Published 2008 by
HERITAGE BOOKS, INC.
Publishing Division
100 Railroad Ave. #104
Westminster, Maryland 21157

Copyright © 2005 Bruce E. Burgoyne and Marie Burgoyne

All rights reserved. No part of this book may be reproduced or transmitted in any form or by any means, electronic or mechanical, including photocopying, recording or by any information storage and retrieval system without written permission from the author, except for the inclusion of brief quotations in a review.

International Standard Book Numbers
Paperbound: 978-0-7884-2565-3
Clothbound: 978-0-7884-7113-1

OTHER HERITAGE BOOKS BY BRUCE E. BURGOYNE:

A Hessian Officer's Diary of the American Revolution Translated From An Anonymous Ansbach-Bayreuth Diary and The Prechtel Diary

Canada During the American Revolutionary War: Lieutenant Friedrich Julius von Papet's Journal of the Sea Voyage to North America and the Campaign Conducted There

CD: Ansbach-Bayreuth Diaries from the Revolutionary War

CD: The Hessian Collection, Vol. 1: Revolutionary War Era

Defeat, Disaster, and Dedication

Diaries of Two Ansbach Jaegers

Diary of a Hessian Grenadier of Colonel Rall's Regiment Written by Johannes Reuber

Eighteenth Century America: (A Hessian Report On the People, the Land, the War) As Noted in the Diary of Chaplain Philipp Waldeck (1776-1780)

Enemy Views: The American Revolutionary War as Recorded by the Hessian Participants

Georg Pausch's Journal and Reports of the Campaign in America, as Translated from the German Manuscript in the Lidgerwood Collection in the Morristown Historical Park Archives, Morristown, NJ

Hesse-Hanau Order Books, A Diary and Roster: A Collection of Items Concerning the Hesse-Hanau Contingent of "Hessians" Fighting Against the American Colonists in the Revolutionary War

Hessian Chaplains: Their Diaries and Duties

OTHER HERITAGE BOOKS BY BRUCE E. BURGOYNE
(continued):

Journal of the Hesse-Cassel Jaeger Corps and Hans Konze's List of Jaeger Officers

Mirbach Order Book: Order Book of the Hesse-Cassel von Mirbach Regiment

Most Illustrious Hereditary Prince: Letters to Their Prince from Members of Hesse-Hanau Military Contingent in the Service of England During the American Revolution

Notes from a British Museum

The Battle of Brandywine, 11 September 1777

The Battle of Guilford Courthouse and the Siege and Surrender at Yorktown by Berthold Koch

The Diary of Lieutenant von Bardeleben and Other von Donop Regiment

The Hesse-Cassel Mirbach Regiment in the American Revolution

The Third English-Waldeck Regiment in the American Revolutionary War

The Trenton Commanders: Johann Gottlieb Rall and George Washington, as noted in Hessian Diaries

Journal of a Hessian Grenadier Battalion

Preface

By the late eighteenth century, continental armies had adopted a unit comprised of men who were familiar with nature, lightly armed, and able to move quickly. They were also excellent marksmen. To fill the ranks of these units, foresters, jaegers in German, chasseurs in French, were recruited and gave the name of their profession to the units - they were jaegers. During the American Revolutionary War, England realized early in the conflict that these units were an ideal solution to the American Indian style of fighting. The two companies of the original Hesse-Cassel contribution to the English effort were quickly increased to a regiment, and the two Ansbach-Bayreuth companies were also increased, before the war's end, to a full regiment.

The *Journal of the Hesse-Cassel Jaeger Corps* was originally published in the *Journal of the Johannes Schwalm Historical Association, Inc* Vol. 3, Nr. 3, 1987; and Vol 3, Nr. 4, 1988. My translation was made from a German language document in the archives of the Morristown National Historical Park, Morristown, NJ. That portion containing excerpts of Captain Johann Hinrichs' diary was published previously in Bernard A. Uhlendorf's *The Siege of Charleston*, University of Michigan Press (Ann Arbor, 1938).

Bruce E. Burgoyne
Dover, DE

Jaeger Corps Journal

Introduction

This version of the Journal of the Hesse-Cassel Jaeger Corps is a translation from a German language copy of the document in the archives of the Morristown National Historical Park, Morristown, NJ. That document appears to be exactly that - a copy - and I have made no effort to determine anything concerning its origin. My translation is unpolished, but should enable researchers to save considerable time in screening the contents. Where the information was readily available, I have added name and unit identification. Some spelling corrections have been made also. In general, the long, involved, and rambling sentences, and often obscure comments of the unknown German journalist have been left as he wrote them.

While the document is not an indispensable account of the Jaeger Corps' activities, it is an excellent, brief, summary of the war. Several of the entries, such as the Hessian intelligence concerning Washington's march from New York to Virginia to besiege Cornwallis, the Benedict Arnold-Major Andre affair, and the naval battle off the Chesapeake Bay, are of special interest. The same may be said of the journalist's comments on the steadily improving quality of the American fighting men.

Jaeger Corps Journal

A large portion of the German version is made up of Captain Hinrich's diary, which was previously translated by Bernard A. Uhlendorf, *The Siege of Charleston with an Account of the Province of South Carolina: Diaries and Letters of Hessian Officers from the Jungkenn Papers in the William L. Clements Library,* University of Michigan Publications, Ann Arbor, 1938.

Other references which were of special value in identifying individuals and units, and verifying dates, places, and activities were: Inge Auergbach and Otto Froehlich (Eds.), *Hessische Truppen in Amerikanischen Unabhaengigkeitskrieg (Hetrina),* 5 vols., Staatsarchiv Marburg, Marburg, Germany; Captain Johann Ewald, *Diary of the American War, A Hessian Journal,* Joseph P. Tustin (Trans. & Ed.), Yale University Press, New Haven, 1979; and Erhard Staedtler, *Die Ansbach-Bayreuther Truppen in Americkanischen Unabhaengigkeitskrieg, 1773-1783,* Gesellschaft fuer Familienforschung in Franken, Nurnberg, Germany, 1956.

Bruce E. Burgoyne
Dover, Delaware

Jaeger Corps Journal

Journal
kept by the
Distinguished Hessian Field Jaeger Corps
During the Campaign
Of the Royal Army of Great Britain
In North America

Begun June 23, 1777, the day on which Lieutenant Colonel Ludwig Johann Adolf von Wurmb assumed command of this Corps and finished on April 20, 1784, upon the successful return of the same royal troops from America.

June 23 - Lieutenant Colonel von Wurmb of the Distinguished Leib [Body] Regiment, today assumed command of the distinguished Field Jaeger Corps, which consisted now of the squadron, dismounted, and the Company of Major [Ernst Carl] von Prueschenck, both of which have just arrived from Europe, and the Companies of [Johann] Ewald and [Carl August] von Wrede, which have already participated in the last campaign, as well as the 105-man company of Ansbach Jaegers commanded by Captain [Christoph August] von Cramon - making in all a force of 600 men - to which a detachment of 1 officer and 30 Hessian grenadiers have been assigned to protect the two 3-pounder cannon attached to the Corps. The army had returned from Braunschweig

Jaeger Corps Journal

[New Jersey] and lay encamped three-quarters of an hour from Amboy. The enemy lay at Morristown.

June 24 - Everything was quiet. Only a few enemy patrols were observed near the posts held by the Jaegers.

June 25 - We received orders to strike our tents at six o'clock in the evening, and be ready to march. About 6 o'clock in the evening, the outposts of the Jaeger Corps, which had about 400 men on duty, were attacked by 400 dismounted and 120 mounted enemy, but beat the enemy back without loss, except for one man who shot himself. The enemy suffered several killed, and we took a number of prisoners.

June 26 - The enemy army advanced as far as Basketreach, in order to attack the rear of our force during the crossing to Staten Island. The royal army advanced therefore, at daybreak, in two columns, to attack the enemy. The right was commanded by [Charles] Lord Cornwallis, and Lieutenant Colonel von Wurmb, with the Companies of von Prueschenck and Wrede, formed the advance guard, which was followed by the Light Infantry. General [Sir William] Howe was with the left column, where Major Prueschenck, with the Companies of Ewald and the Ansbachers were the advance guard. Several skirmishes occurred, involving the right column - the Jaegers and Light Infantry driving the enemy from some heights, without significant loss, in that the

Jaeger Corps Journal

Light Infantry had only a few killed and wounded. The English Guards and the Hessian Minnigerode Grenadier Battalion attacked an enemy post, and the Guards captured one cannon and the Grenadiers, two cannons. At evening the army camped near Westfield. General Howe reconnoitered the enemy positions at Basketreach and found them too strong, so on

June 27 - he marched back to Rahway. The enemy followed with small parties and, as the march was very tiring and the heat exceptionally great, we lost several men who died of the heat, in particular four men of the Squadron who had marched on foot.

June 28 - The army marched to Amboy today, as the general had decided to leave this desolate province, and already by afternoon, some troops had crossed over to Staten Island.

June 29 - The army was engaged today in crossing to Staten Island. The enemy did not interfere.

June 30 - The army rear guard, consisting of the Grenadiers, the Light Infantry, and the Jaegers, all left the province of Jersey, today, without interference, and camped with the army on Staten Island.

July 1 - The army moved to a camp on the heights of Staten Island (the right flank against the Flagstaff) and received orders to be ready to embark on an exercise, furnished with provisions.

July 9 - Today the last troops went aboard the transport ships, ending the embarkation, but the fleet

Jaeger Corps Journal

with the troops on board, nevertheless, lay until

July 20 - when the anchors were raised and the fleet sailed to Sandy Hook, where it anchored again, so that everything which was a part of the fleet could be brought together.

July 21 & 22 - The wind was contrary and the fleet could not depart.

July 23 - We sailed this morning with a favorable wind and set course for the Delaware, or so we think. We had good weather, but not the best wind. Nevertheless, we reached the mouth of the Delaware on

July 30 - and believed certainly, that we would be landed at New Castle, but we sailed no further than Cape Henlopen, where we met the *Roebuck*, of 40-guns [Sir Snape Hammond] on its assigned station.

July 31 - To our utter amazement, the fleet departed from Delaware Bay, and put to sea. Sir Snape Hammond is said to have caused this, in that he claimed the area around New Castle is too dangerous, because of the many enemy fire-ships which can be sent against the fleet. The fleet set a course for the Chesapeake, which is normally a two-day journey, but contrary winds delayed us until

Aug. 15 - when the fleet came to anchor at Cape Henry. On

Aug. 16 - we anchored at Milford

Aug. 17 - by Queen's Island

Jaeger Corps Journal

Aug. 18 - near Schmitspoint
Aug. 19 - near Cedarpoint
Aug. 20 - between Wards and Sharps Islands
Aug. 21 - near Bodkinspoint
Aug. 22 - near Turkeypoint, opposite Georgetown, and really so close to the land of Chester County, that the fleet could very easily have been fired upon.
Aug. 23 & 24 - The necessary arrangements were made for debarking.
Aug. 25 - This morning at three o'clock, the debarkation began, in the following order:

1st Debarkation

The Jaeger Corps first; the 1st and 2nd Battalions of Light Infantry; the 1st and 2nd Battalions of English Grenadiers

2nd Debarkation

Hessian Grenadiers, Queen's Rangers, English Guards, 4th and 23rd Regiments

3rd Debarkation

28th, 49th, 5th, 10th, 27th, 40th, 55th, 15th, and 42nd Regiments

4th Debarkation

44th, 17th, 33rd, 37th, 46th, 64th, and 71st Regiments

5th Debarkation

[The Hessian Regiments] Leib, Donop, and Mirbach; the Combined Battalion; and the Artillery and Cavalry of the army

The landing was conducted in the most orderly

Jaeger Corps Journal

fashion at Elk Ferry, near Turkeypoint (which is a narrow peninsula) with a single narrow exit toward Elktown, a small town of about 40 houses, on the river of this name. As soon as the 1st Division landed, and because there were no reports of enemy activity, the men were immediately formed by companies, without regard to seniority, in order to be prepared to resist the certainly nearby enemy, and to cover the landing of the entire army, but no enemy appeared.

 Aug. 26 & 27 - The army remained in place while the necessary baggage was put ashore, and everything made ready for the march.

 Aug. 28 - The army departed Turkeypoint and marched to Elktown, which had been deserted by all the inhabitants. We had no reports about the enemy, and no maps of the interior of this land, and no one in the army was familiar with this area. After we had passed the city, no one knew which way to go. Therefore, men were sent out in all directions until finally a Negro was found, and the army had to march according to his directions. This Negro knew nothing about the enemy army, himself, but said that a corps of the same was reported to be in the area, and some of their scouting parties were seen by the Jaeger Corps, which constituted the advance guard. The army made camp in the woods. The Jaeger Corps made camp at the foot of a hill, on which the Light Infantry was posted. We remained lying here until September 3,

Jaeger Corps Journal

and meantime took several prisoners from the frequently observed scouting parties. They told us that the enemy army was not nearby, as we had otherwise thought, but that a corps of 1,200 men, an elite group, was at Iron Hill. (This is the highest point between Chesapeake Bay and Philadelphia.)

Sept. 3 - Major General [James] Grant remained with six battalions at Elk, in order to maintain communications with the ships. At daybreak, Lord Cornwalllis' column broke camp and marched to Cecil Courthouse, where Lieutenant General [Wilhelm, Freiherr] von Knyphausen joined with it. The Jaegers, consisting of the Companies of Prueschenck, Wrede, Ewald, and Ansbach, in all about four hundred men, were the advance guard, and learned during the march that enemy pickets had been there. Indications were that the enemy had marched off to the left. Colonel von Wurmb had this reported, and requested orders as to which direction he should march. Sir William Howe himself came up and ordered that the enemy be followed. After half an hour, our flankers saw the enemy's rear. The mounted jaegers engaged them at once, and Captain Ewald, who led the Corps' advance guard, soon came under fire. Then we saw the enemy, consisting of about one thousand men, as they marched into a thin woods. The Jaeger Corps deployed from the middle, to right and left, and formed so that the Ansbachers were in the middle, the point which the enemy at once attacked. They were driven back into another woods, with considerable effort. Here they defended themselves obstinately, which brought our right wing, under Captain Wrede, with the hanger [saber] to the attack. We also drove the enemy from this place, and they took a third position behind the Cutgers Bridge. This however, only in order to better cover their retreat, which they made into a heavy woods, without stopping to make a stand again. Now, and only after the enemy had retreated, a battalion of light infantry joined us for the first time, which General Howe had detached from the right to support us, but which could not get through a morass, and the 2nd Battalion, detached from the left, could not reach us because of a large swamp. Therefore, the Jaeger Corps fought this enemy corps all by itself, and the commanding general officially thanked Lieutenant Colonel von Wurmb and the entire corps in orders. We buried between thirty and forty of the enemy dead, not counting those concealed by the bushes.

Our loss was one dead and fifteen wounded Hessians, and four wounded Ansbachers. The army then camped. The Jaegers had their posts on the left flank in a very pleasant, but exposed woods.

A captain, and whenever possible, two subalterns, with seventy and often one hundred men, now and during the entire campaign, manned the various

Jaeger Corps Journal

pickets of the Corps, and this force then became the advance or rear guard, whenever march resumed. The picket force was relieved every 24 hours. The Corps itself was often alarmed by false or real alerts during the night, and often had to stand to arms. Therefore, every jaeger, just as if he were in formation, had to lie down with his weapon in his arms, and each time, at the least alarm, was immediately ready to respond, which then also, in every instance, seemed to be required. The cavalry camped each time at a certain distance behind the infantry and was always saddled, and for the most part, mounted. The tents and heavy baggage of the army at this point were put aboard the ships.

Sept. 6 - Major General Grant with his six battalions rejoined the army. The royal fleet had left the Elk River, and those enemy vehicles which could not be taken away, were burned.

Sept. 8 - The enemy army moved forward as far as Newark, and was so situated that the right wing rested on, or more to the point, was covered by Christiana Creek, and the left on Red Clay Creek. The army marched there today, in the following order:

1st Division. Lord Cornwallis - Jaegers, 1st and 2nd Battalions of Light Infantry, English Grenadiers, Hessian Grenadiers, the Guards.

2nd Division. Major General Grant - Two squadrons of the 16th Dragoons, 1st Brigade of

Artillery, 1st and 2nd Brigades of English Infantry, 3rd Brigade of Artillery, 3rd and 4th Brigades of English Infantry - finally the army train.

Jaeger Corps Journal

3rd Division. Lieutenant General von Knyphausen - the dismounted jaegers of the squadron, 2nd Brigade of Artillery, General Stirn's Brigade of Hessians, 1st Squadron of the 16th Dragoons, 40th Regiment, two 3-pounders, 71st Regiment, Queen's Rangers, the English Jaegers.

The 3rd Battalion of the 71st Regiment covered the right flanks of the baggage. At evening, the army camped on the road to Newark, not far from Hockessin, a distance of four miles from the enemy.

Sept. 9 - Yesterday and during the past night, the enemy moved along the road toward Wilmington, having passed over the Brandywine Creek near Chadds Ford, and taken post on the heights nearby, and begun to throw up redoubts, also. This movement caused the royal army to draw together, in that Lieutenant General von Knyphausen marched to New Garden and Kennet Square, and Lord Cornwallis marched to Hockessin Meeting House, and both were united the next morning,

Sept. 10 - at Kennet Square.

Sept. 11 - At daybreak, the army moved forward in two columns, the right under Lieutenant General von Knyphausen, including Major General Grant, took the road to Chadds Ford, seven miles from Kennet Square, and arrived at ten o'clock in front of the enemy. The advance guard of this column, consisting of the Queen's Rangers, skirmished with the enemy outposts

Jaeger Corps Journal

as the column moved into position, and as General von Knyphausen was not to attack before the left column, under Sir William Howe and Lord Cornwallis, attacked the enemy's right wing, he engaged the enemy only with artillery fire, as if he intended to force the ford. Meantime, Sir William Howe marched to the first arm of the Brandywine Creek, a distance of twelve miles. The jaegers were the advance guard for this column, and were supported by the 1st and 2nd Battalions of Light Infantry, commanded by Lieutenant Colonel [Robert] Abercromby. These were followed by the grenadiers. Captain Ewald, with fifty jaegers, supported by Captain [William] Scott with his company of light infantry, had the most advanced position before the Jaeger Corps. About two miles this side of the Brandywine, we met an enemy patrol of one hundred men, which retreated into the woods, leaving a few prisoners behind. This force was the one which notified General [George] Washington of our approach, and convinced him to change his belief, which up till now, was that our army really intended to cross at Chadds Ford, and to detach the largest part of his army to oppose us.

Meanwhile, we crossed the first arm of the Brandywine Creek at Tinckloss Ford, and the second at Jeffreys Ford. Here was such a high hill, that five hundred men with two cannon, could have made

Jaeger Corps Journal

passage impossible, or at least extremely difficult, and since this was not occupied, the general was reinforced in his belief that Washington wanted to retreat and did not wish a battle. Further, that it was not his wish to engage, but that Congress had given him positive orders to attack It was extremely difficult to move the artillery over the height, and therefore the column halted on the opposite side of the height until two o'clock. After the artillery had been brought over and we could resume our march in columns, in this rather open area, Captain Ewald, about three o'clock, reported the enemy army was marching toward us. Thereupon we received orders to form in line. The advance guard deployed from the middle to the right and left. The Jaeger Corps had the honor to man the extreme left wing, and consisted, after the departure of the detachments under Captain Ewald and the cavalry, which because of the difficult terrain, could not follow us, of something over three hundred men with two English 3-pounders, which were covered by the Hessian Jaeger Lieutenant Balthasar Mertz with thirty grenadiers, but during the advance had to be left behind with the grenadiers. The Hessian Grenadiers supported the right wing, and the 3rd Brigade of Englanders likewise was to support the Jaegers and Light Infantry in the second encounter, but because of the uneven terrain and the movement toward the left by the column, we saw nothing of it

Jaeger Corps Journal

during the battle. About three-thirty, the Jaeger Corps found itself close to an enemy advance post, with two 6-pounders and six hundred men, which stood on a height, with a woods in front of it. Our two 3-pounders opened fire first, the Jaegers attacked the enemy, drove them into a bush, and dislodged them three different times, before they retreated back to the main body of the army. The main army was advantageously posted on a not especially steep height in front of a woods, with the right wing resting on a steep and deep ravine. This wing was directly opposite the Jaegers, and in the same bushes from which the Jaegers had driven the enemy corps; and the Jaegers were engaged for over half an hour, with grape shot and small arms, with a battalion of light infantry. We could not see the 2nd Battalion of Light Infantry because of the terrain, and while we received only a few orders, each commander had to act according to his own best judgment. Meanwhile, the firing became more general and stronger, and Lieutenant Colonel von Wurmb heard that the right wing was advancing. Therefore, he had the call to attack sounded on the half moon [hunting horn], and the Jaegers, with the battalion of light infantry, stormed up the height. The enemy retreated in confusion, abandoning two cannon and an ammunition cassion, which the Light Infantry, because they had attacked on the less steep slope of the height, took possession of. We had no cavalry, our

Jaeger Corps Journal

people were very fatigued, and in only a moment, the enemy were out of sight. Therefore, we made no prisoners. The Jaegers lost Lieutenant Forster of Ansbach, and six men killed, as well as Hessian Jaeger Captain [Johann Friedrich] Trautwetter, 3 sergeants, and 35 men severely wounded. Of these the first, and many of the latter, died. The losses by the Light Infantry were not as great, and of the enemy we saw many dead and wounded. Thereafter, as the 2nd Battalion of Light Infantry had attacked so far to the right, we stood at a great distance from the army, and not until about seven o'clock in the evening, on orders, were we rejoined to the army at Dilworth, where they had encamped on the battlefield, rather than continuing in pursuit of the enemy. Lieutenant General von Knyphausen, according to the agreed upon plan, had advanced over Chadds Ford as soon as he heard firing on our front, taking three cannon and a howitzer in a small redoubt, which was overrun, and also forced the enemy into flight. The total losses to the royal army is about four hundred dead and wounded.

The enemy, on the other hand, is figured to have had three hundred killed, six hundred wounded, and four hundred taken prisoner.

Sept. 12 - General Howe thanked the army for its part in yesterday's battle in official orders, and especially those troops of the advance guard who participated in the initial assault. To our complete surprise, the army remained quiet, with only Major General Grant with the 1st and 2nd Brigades moving to Concord.

Sept. 13 - The Jaegers marched on the left front of the army. Lord Cornwallis, with the Light Infantry and the Grenadiers, joined Major General Grant, and moved to within five miles of Chester, where a part of the enemy was reportedly entrenched. The 71st Regiment therefore was detached to dislodge them, and establish a post there, but upon arrival found the place already clear of the enemy.

Sept. 14 - Today the sick and wounded of the army were sent to Wilmington, escorted by Colonel [Johann August] von Loos with the Combined Battalion. The Jaegers sent a patrol to Renny, where they took a few prisoners, and destroyed a small magazine.

Sept. 15 - Everything quiet. Orders to march tomorrow.

Sept. 16 - The Mirbach Regiment marched to Wilmington to provide protection for the hospital. The army marched to the left, to attack General Washington, who was marching on the road toward Lancaster, according to reports received. The Jaegers and Light Infantry fell in with these forces and had sharp skirmishes.

One captain, one officer, and twenty men of the enemy force were captured and many left [dead] on

Jaeger Corps Journal

the battlefield. On our side, one man was killed and several wounded. Because of especially rainy weather, however, the march was not continued, and camp was set up near Butte [Boot Tavern?]. The enemy also, as a result of the rain, camped at Black Horse [White Horse?], postponing his march.

Sept. 17 - General Howe's column remained in camp, but Lord Cornwallis advanced along the Lancaster Road and established a post two miles distant from Lieutenant General von Knyphausen.

Sept. 18 - The army joined together today on the Lancaster Road near White Horse. We learned that the enemy had crossed the Schuylkill and was encamped on both sides of the Perkgomy River

Sept. 19 - All quiet. Orders to march tomorrow.

Sept. 20 - The army marched in the following order: Jaegers in front, Light Infantry, 1st, 2nd, 3rd, and 4th Brigades of English, Stirn's Hessian Brigade, Hessian Grenadiers, and the Dragoons, which like the Artillery, were divided into detachments and placed in front of the brigades. The Queen's Rangers and two battalions of English [?] covered the flanks. The Jaeger Corps skirmished continuously during the march. Camp was established at Valley Forge, where several magazines, a cannon foundry, and a ruined weapons factory were located.

Sept. 21 - The past night, Major General [Charles] Gray, with the Light Infantry, the 42nd and 44th

Jaeger Corps Journal

Regiments, were detached in order to surprise an enemy corps of 1,500 men under General [Anthony] Wayne, which stood alone in a woods. He reached the enemy at one o'clock in the night, broke in the left flank, with unloaded weapons, killed and wounded three hundred men, took eighty prisoners, and the greatest part of the baggage, as well as many weapons, but the enemy had taken their cannon away. The English loss was one captain and three men killed, and four wounded.

The army broke camp very early and marched in the following order: Jaegers, Light Infantry, Hessian Grenadiers, three brigades of artillery, the army baggage and train, the 4th, 2nd, and 1st English Brigades. The 3rd Brigade covered the flanks and the Hessian Brigade served as the rear guard. The army continued up to the bank of the Schuylkill, and the camp extended from Falland Ford to the French Creek. Therefore the enemy left his location and marched to Pottsgrove. The Jaegers and the Light Infantry, as usual during the march, skirmished with the enemy at every defile and woods.

Sept. 22 - Sixty jaegers and one hundred grenadiers, under the command of Captain von Wrede, crossed the Schulylkill over Falland Ford this afternoon, and seized several outposts in order to mask the main river crossing. The army during the night, resumed its march. Lord Cornwallis

Jaeger Corps Journal

commanded the advance guard (the Jaegers at the head of the same) and crossed the river at Chadds Ford, where the entire army crossed without meeting any resistance. Captain von Wrede then re-crossed the river and rejoined the army, which by morning was already encamped with the left wing resting on the Schuylkill. The 2nd Battalion of Light Infantry was detached to Swedes Ford where the enemy had left six spiked, iron cannon.

Sept. 24 - All quiet. General Washington had pulled back to Schibbach Creek. We received orders to march tomorrow morning at daybreak.

Sept. 25 - The army marched to Germantown in two columns and entered camp already set up there by the Guards of the right wing. This wing contained General Grant's Brigade, the Rangers, and the Light Infantry in the advance corps, supported by the Dragoons. The center had the English Infantry, in whose front at Germantown, the 40th Regiment and the 1st Battalion of Light Infantry held the advance posts. The left wing consisting of the Hessians and the Jaeger Corps stood on the road to Lancaster, from Philadelphia. The Minnigerode Grenadier Battalion was posted so as to support the Jaegers at a place known by the name of Schuylkill Falls.

Sept. 26 - Lord Cornwallis marched at eight o'clock this morning with the English and Hessian Grenadiers toward Philadelphia, which had already

Jaeger Corps Journal

been evacuated by the enemy and the Congress for some time. Cornwallis occupied the city during the afternoon, in order to protect it from the enemy ships lying in the Delaware River, and threw up three batteries for six 12-pounders. These were still not completed when on

Sept 27 - two frigates and several other armed ships came from Mud Island and attacked the lower battery of two cannon. The largest frigate of 30-guns, called the *Delaware*, anchored five hundred rods from the battery and the others, somewhat further away. At ten o'clock they began to bombard the city as well as the batteries, with a heavy fire, but as the ebb set in, the *Delaware* ran aground. The four cannon of the Grenadier Battalion were then turned on the ship, and so well directed that it struck, and was occupied by a company of Englanders. The remaining craft, after the frigate was lost, returned to their former station at Mud Island.

Sept. 28 - Nearly all the residents have left Philadelphia. The enemy have very strongly fortified Mud Island, which is an island in the Delaware some miles below Philadelphia, and this disrupts the communications by water, which because of provisions, is absolutely necessary for us. In addition to this island and the works on the Jersey shore, the enemy has many ships to aid their defenses. Also the river is barricaded by chevaux de frise against the

Jaeger Corps Journal

entry of our ship, so that it will be necessary for us to formally besiege the place in order to open the communications, to which end, the necessarily preparations are already well under way.

Oct. 1 - During the past night, the 10th and 42nd Regiments occupied a fortification at Billingsport, which is in Jersey, on the bank of the Delaware, and cover the chevaux de frise in the river before Mud Island. The enemy offered no resistance and had spiked the cannon. Our ships at once began to dismantle the lower chevaux de frise. On the other hand, the enemy worked diligently on Mud Island and the fort opposite, at Red Bank.

Oct. 4 - The many detachments which General Howe had sent to Philadelphia and into the Jerseys to besiege and occupy the city caused General Washington to consider a movement, especially since being strengthened from Virginia, to attack the royal army. With this in mind, he broke camp at Schibbach Creek, and about two o'clock in the morning, we received reports of his approach. Lieutenant Colonel von Wurmb immediately moved out with the Jaeger Corps, reported the attack to General von Knyphausen, and occupied the bridge over the Wissahickon, near the Vanderen's house.

Shortly thereafter, one heard firing on the right wing, and about three-thirty, the Jaeger Corps was attacked by a corps of four thousand men with four 6-

pounders. Our Corps had to give up the bridge, but took position on a height opposite and defended it with rifle fire against the enemy's repeated attempts to force a crossing. The four enemy cannon fired continuously upon the jaegers, while our 3-pounders could not reach the enemy. The firing meantime became general, and very heavy on the right wing, until about nine o'clock, when Lieutenant General von Knyphausen reported the enemy's left wing turned back. At this, Lieutenant Colonel von Wurmb attacked the bridge again, and drove this enemy away, and also away from the opposite heights, with a withering fire. As the attack had to be continued through a long defile, the enemy had time to retire. Therefore we found only twenty dead and, as the jaegers were much fatigued, without support, and were only three hundred men, there was no further pursuit.

In the center of the army, the enemy had attacked the Light Infantry and driven it back. Lieutenant Colonel [Thomas] Musgrave threw himself and the 40th Regiment into a stone house, which the enemy then attacked. As a result, the enemy was held up, instead of being able to press his main attack, before our entire army took up arms. The army counter-attacked the enemy and drove them out of the city, and into flight. They retreated to their previous camp on the Schibbach Creek, leaving behind three hundred dead, six hundred wounded, and four hundred prisoners. Our losses were near four hundred dead and wounded, among the first, General [James] Agnew.

Lord Cornwallis in Philadelphia had heard the firing, and at once ordered three grenadier battalions to march from that place. He alone arrived soon enough to take part in the action, but the battalions were too late.

Oct. 5 - Yesterday our fleet from the Chesapeake arrived in the Delaware, not far from New Castle, and will now be employed to capture Mud Island as soon as possible, in order finally to open communications, and thereby at least, simplify the delivery of provisions.

Presently only small boats are able to bring the most necessary supplies past the enemy ships stationed there.

Oct. 6 - The enemy works on Mud Island consist of a fort with four block houses, two floating batteries, one of nine cannon, fourteen galleys with heavy cannon, and numerous other vessels. Directly opposite in Jersey lies Red Bank, which covers the ships, and before which the chevaux de frise in the river prevent the entrance of our ships.

Reports from New York are to the effect that on August 22, the enemy, under General [William] Smallwood, landed on Staten Island and overran two provincial regiments, which occupied the outposts,

Jaeger Corps Journal

and had not been alert.

Upon receiving the alarm, English troops under Brigadier General [John] Campbell moved out to attack the enemy. They made contact, and engaged the enemy at one o'clock, just as they were about to retreat into their boats. About three hundred of the enemy fell into English hands.

Jaeger Corps Journal

On Sept. 12, General [Sir Henry] Clinton went into Jersey with some of the troops from York Island, annoyed the enemy, and created a diversion in favor of General Howe as well as General [Sir John] Burgoyne. The militia gave the general some resistance. He remained there until September 16, sending back much livestock during that time, for the benefit of the hospital.

On Sept. 27, a fleet with provisions and recruits arrived at New York, among which were the two new jaeger companies of [Philipp] von Wurmb and [Friederich Henrich] Lorey. Therefore, General Clinton immediately made preparations to proceed up the North River toward General Burgoyne.

Oct. 19 - The army broke camp at Germantown today and marched to Philadelphia, entering a camp on the heights before the town, near Morris House, in order to be nearer to, and to support the operations against Mud Island.

Oct. 21 - Colonel [Carl Emil Kurt] von Donop with the Jaeger Corps, the Grenadier Brigade, and the Mirbach Regiment crossed the Delaware today near Philadelphia, and landed at Coopers Ferry in order to capture Fort Red Bank. He marched to Haddonfield and established posts there, toward evening.

Oct. 22 - About four o'clock this morning, these troops broke camp and marched over Strawberrybank

Jaeger Corps Journal

against Fort Red Bank, and about midday they arrived within a quarter of a mile of the fort. The enemy had received reports of the approach of the troops, and had set to work to improve his defenses. The fort was at once called upon to surrender, and as the officer commanding therein, Colonel [Christopher] Green, would not give up, preparations were begun to storm the fort. The attack began at four o'clock in the afternoon and continued until dusk, but to no avail, because the walls were too high and there were no ladders available. The Jaeger Corps covered both flanks to the water, to prevent a landing from the ships, which nevertheless, did the force considerable damage with their cannon. Colonel von Donop was fatally wounded at the edge of the moat, and therefore did not desire being brought back. He fell into enemy hands.

The troops, after having advanced as far as the moat under heavy fire, found the defenses impossible to surmount, and retreated. The Jaeger Corps formed the rear guard for some distance, then half formed the advance guard in order to capture the bridge over Timber Creek, in case it should be occupied by the enemy. The enemy remained quietly in the fort, and our entire force camped on the far side of Timber Creek, returning

Oct. 23 - over Haddonfield and crossed the Delaware the same day and again returned to camp with the army. Several warships were to have supported the attack on the fort, but because of contrary winds, could not approach near enough. The following day, namely the 23rd, the 64-gun ship *Augusta* and two frigates ran onto the chevaux de frise and stuck fast.

After this unfortunate affair, batteries were thrown up with great difficultly in the bogs of Province Island, and initially on

Nov. 10 - began firing, but basically with little effect.

Nov. 15 - The wind was favorable today and especially as there was a spring tide (when the water is a foot or more higher, and this only occurs by every changing phase of the moon), it was possible to employ the ships against Mud Island. The *Agilant*, a 24-gun ship, with sixteen 24-pounders, sailed with a sloop with three 24-pounders, under Lieutenant Hotham, through the channel between Province and Hog Islands, against the fort. There was a heavy cannonade which did great damage to the enemy, and forced him on

Nov. 16 - to abandon the fort and the island during the night. The enemy set fire to his ships and retreated to Jersey. If this had not occurred, the English Guards had already been ordered to storm the fort. The English Grenadiers occupied the fort. Reportedly the enemy loss during the siege amounted to about four

Jaeger Corps Journal

hundred dead and wounded. The King's losses were seven dead and five wounded.

Nov. 17 - Yesterday, a fleet arrived in the Delaware at Chester, which General Clinton, after General Burgoyne's capture and the expedition up the North River was to no avail, had sent to General Howe as a reinforcement.

The report of that misfortune is the following:

Following the arrival at New York on September 27 of the fleet from England, General Clinton went up the North River on October 1. On October 6, he captured Forts Montgomery and Clinton, which were situated on the two banks of the river. This occurred about six o'clock in the afternoon, by storming the forts. The Trumbach Regiment and the two jaeger companies newly arrived from Germany, participated. After the forts on both sides had been captured, the enemy set fire to both of his frigates, *Montgomery* and *Congress,* and several other vessels, and retired up the river. Fort Constitution, which lay somewhat farther up river, was called upon to surrender, and as it refused, a detachment was sent to storm the fort on October 7. As this force approached however, the enemy abandoned the fort.

More than one hundred cannon and considerable war material were taken from the enemy during this period.

General [John] Vaughan went up the river with a

Jaeger Corps Journal

detachment aboard Sir James Wallace's ships, and landed on October 15 at Aesopus, which some of the enemy had fortified. These were attacked, most were captured, and the city was burned. Then this corps sailed further up river with the intent of opening communications with General Burgoyne, and to make contact with him. Unfortunately however, the project was in vain, as news came that General Burgoyne had surrendered as prisoners of war at Saratoga, on October 16. Upon being convinced of this misfortune, the force returned to Montgomery, which place was closed down also, and at once evacuated. The troops arrived back at New York already on October 24, and were at once put aboard ship, and arrived at the Delaware on November 9.

Nov. 18 - Lord Cornwallis marched out of camp at Philadelphia tonight with fifty jaegers (Captain von Wrede), a battalion of light infantry, an English [grenadier battalion], and the [Hessian] Lengercke Grenadier Battalion, as well as the 33rd Regiment, and on the nineteenth, crossed the Delaware near Chester, where he joined with those forces at Billingsport, and with the troops already landed from New York, which were under Major General [Sir Thomas Spencer] Wilson.

Nov. 21 - Lord Cornwallis' force, consisting of the above corps, marched to conquer Red Bank, which after the loss of Mud Island, was still in enemy hands,

Jaeger Corps Journal

and under [the protection of] whose cannon, several enemy ships had retreated. Cornwallis marched over Mende Bridge and camped near Woodbury, where he received news that the enemy had vacated the fort, and set fire to all his ships. Therefore, the general detached the English Grenadiers to occupy the fort.

Nov. 24 - This corps marched to the region of Red Bank.

Nov. 25 - The march resumed today to Gloucester, at which place the corps re-crossed the Delaware and rejoined the army. While the necessary preparations were being made for the crossing, the detachment of jaegers under Captain von Wrede, were posted to cover the crossing. About four o'clock in the afternoon, an enemy corps under General Green, came from Mount Holly and attacked, but was repulsed after a hot engagement, in which both parties alternately retreated, until at dusk, the enemy pulled back. The loss for the Jaegers was one officer and four dead men, one officer and thirteen men wounded, and ten men missing. The enemy loss could not be determined, as he took off the dead and wounded, except for one dead officer.

Nov. 26 - The entire corps crossed the Delaware, with only a few enemy causing interference, and rejoined the army in camp at Philadelphia, having finally opened the communications on the Delaware, which had cost considerable time, effort, and men.

Jaeger Corps Journal

The enemy losses were estimated at one 32-pounder, one 24-pounder, seven 18-pounders, and one 12-pounder at Mud Island; six 18-pounders, three 12-pounders, two 6-pounders, and five 4-pounders at Red Bank; and between three and four hundred dead and wounded.

While all these operations on the Delaware were transpiring, General Washington remained quietly in his camp at White Marsh, not far from Germantown, while he meanwhile fortified it with an abatis and several redoubts, and called in a reinforcement from the northern army.

Dec. 4 - The army marched tonight at eleven o'clock, in two columns, toward Germantown and, because it was night and dark, the Light Infantry served as the advance guard, followed by the Jaegers. The enemy outposts skirmished continuously during the advance, and at daybreak the army reached Chestnut Hill, and marched to the front of the enemy's right wing. The Jaeger Corps took its post on the left wing, opposite the enemy's right. The Light Infantry was posted about the middle of the army, also in an advance position. About nine o'clock, a corps of about three hundred men from the enemy's right wing, moved to a position on a height lying opposite the Jaeger Corps, so that the two groups began firing at one another. Toward eleven o'clock, the enemy detached another corps of about one thousand men,

Jaeger Corps Journal

which attacked the Light Infantry posted in front of the center of the line, but pulled back after a brief exchange of fire. The enemy lost many people in this action and many, including the commander of the corps, were captured.

Dec. 6 - The corps, which had been posted opposite the Jaeger Corps, pulled back during the night without having taken any action, except sending out a few patrols, which wounded three of our men. The two armies stood face to face, the enemy on a height protected by an abatis and a redoubt. Washington appeared to be awaiting an attack and stood his ground.

General Howe believed the enemy position here to be too strong, and wanted to test the left wing, so the army left this area, and marched on Dec. 7 - off to the right to Abington Township, toward the enemy's left flank, where it arrived during the afternoon, and placed itself before the enemy. It was necessary to dislodge an enemy advance corps before our army could make camp. Therefore, the Jaeger Corps was ordered to do this. We found the enemy on a steep height, very advantageously posted. The Corps marched against this position in a frontal attack and drove the enemy back nearly into the abatis. It was a corps of the so-called riflemen, recently arrived from Canada, which had united with General Washington's army, and consisted of about five hundred men. As

Jaeger Corps Journal

our cavalry had to contend with the enemy, we only took thirty prisoners, and we had three killed and nine wounded, while the enemy lost about twenty killed. Following this action, the army encamped. The Jaeger Corps being posted very near the enemy, the pickets continuously fired upon one another.

Dec. 8 - Completely against all expectations, today the army marched back to Philadelphia, because the general found the enemy positions too strong to attack. The return march was uneventful. The Jaegers formed the rear guard, which was kept under observation by several cavalrymen.

Dec. 10 - Lord Cornwallis crossed the Schuylkill with 3,600 men, in order to gather forage. The advance guard of this corps, consisting of a detachment of jaegers (Captain Crammon), both mounted and dismounted, and light infantry. They encountered an enemy party, capturing part and completely dispersing the rest. Cornwallis advanced as far as Swedes Ford, where he met the enemy marching on the other side of the Schuylkill, toward a camp at Valley Forge. The enemy, believing the king's army planned to attack, drew up in line of battle. Cornwallis amused himself at the enemy's expense all day, but on

Dec. 11 - returned to Philadelphia because he had accomplished his mission of obtaining forage. During his retreat, he was not harassed.

Jaeger Corps Journal

Dec. 13 - Reports are current that General Washington has actually made his camp at Valley Forge, and is having huts constructed for use during the winter.

Dec. 22 - General Howe took the entire army across the Schuylkill, and extended the left wing to the far side of Darby, with the object of obtaining forage. The enemy army remained very quiet, and only the light troops were nearly constantly skirmishing. The Jaegers had the outposts before the right wing, and several were wounded.

Dec. 27 - A heavy snow fell, completely snowing in the army, which camped without tents or huts.

Dec. 29 - The enemy marched back to its former camp at Philadelphia. The Jaegers formed the rear guard, and were followed by an enemy party which failed, however, to do any harm.

Dec. 30 - The army went into winter quarters in the city of Philadelphia. The Jaegers were centered in the so-called Philadelphia Neck, which is the peninsula between the Delaware and Schuylkill Rivers.

The winter quarters, although the armies were not far apart, and especially because everyone believed that the enemy camp was much exposed, against everything that was to be expected, and no less to our amazement, remained very quiet. The king's army had

Jaeger Corps Journal

very pleasant quarters, and were protected by eleven redoubts, which formed a chain from the Delaware, over Morris Heights, to the Schuylkill. Each of these redoubts was occupied by a captain with fifty men, who were relieved every 24 hours. Pickets of provincials were posted on the banks of the Schuylkill, and the Jaegers had two pickets on the Delaware, at the so-called Hollands Ferry, and at Greenwich Point. The enemy was at Valley Forge, where he had built huts in which to spend the winter.

The many deserters who came in to us, and all the reports which we received, indicated the enemy army was in dire straights, and in particular, equipment, salt, and alcoholic beverages were lacking, and that the shortage in these necessities resulted in dreadful illnesses. On the other hand, the army had everything necessary, is healthy, and although the enemy does everything possible to cut us off from fresh provisions, there are no shortages, but everything is exceptionally expensive.

Jaeger Corps Journal

1778

Mar. 12 - A small detachment of Englanders went up both sides of the Delaware on foraging command and brought back a quantity of hay, without encountering any opposition.

Several scouting parties were sent out from Philadelphia, consisting of raw, newly-enrolled provincials who used their military role for plundering. However, they never made serious contact with the enemy, unless rich booty was to be expected.

Mar. 15 - Upon news that an enemy party had the daring, close on the opposite bank of the Schuylkill, to demand contributions from a resident there, Lieutenant Mertz and the mounted Jaegers were ordered to follow them. They made contact and attacked, capturing one captain and ten men, killed several, and the remainder saved themselves, escaping through the woods. The enemy detachment had consisted of some eighty men.

Mar. 27 - A transport ship, *Brilliant,* coming from New York with convalescents and baggage on board, had the misfortune of grounding near Philadelphia during a strong wind storm. All the personnel were saved, but the baggage was lost.

Now we hear of the peace overtures from Parliament. Everyone was so completely convinced that peace would result, and so certain had this belief taken hold, that we were astounded and amazed by

Jaeger Corps Journal

Congress' scornful refusal of everything which in the least curtailed independence.

Apr. 1 - Because the enemy prevented, for the most part, all the people who wished, from bringing their produce to market, not only taking their produce but also greatly mistreating the people, Lieutenant Colonel von Wurmb ordered the Jaeger Corps to march out three times a week to prevent this, and to give the people protection. This accomplished the wished-for-effect, although these expeditions were very dangerous, and had to be undertaken with the greatest care, because the region was densely occupied, and for the most part, covered with woods. But even more so, because the enemy always knew before hand the time when we would march out, and that we could not be supported by the line units at any great distance. Nevertheless, it never came to a serious engagement, although we always expected such when we marched out. Initially we encountered small, but evermore frequent skirmishes.

May 4 - All the Hessian troops passed in revue before the commanding general, who expressed his satisfaction with the proper military appearance of the men.

May 7 - Some armed brigantines and schooners went up the Delaware and burned the enemy frigates *Washington* and *Effingham*, as well as a 24-gun ship and several smaller vessels which lay at Burlington.

Some houses and a magazine with all sorts of war materials were also burned, which ended this expedition.

May 8 - Sir Henry Clinton arrived in Philadelphia today to assume command of the army as General Howe has been recalled to England.

May 13 - A frigate entered Philadelphia, bringing the unexpected rumor that France had recognized the Americans' independence, and signed a treaty with them.

May 14 - The army was ordered to equip itself as lightly as possible for taking the field, and to deliver up all heavy baggage.

May 19 - An enemy command of six thousand men under [Maria Joseph] Marquis de Lafayette approached the line before Philadelphia, advancing as far as Whitemarsh and Chestnut Hill. Therefore, a large corps was detached from the army this evening to march to the Schuylkill, and whenever possible, to engage the army. A jaeger detachment, commanded by Captain Ewald, constituted the advance guard.

May 20 - The army under Lieutenant General von Knyphausen marched out this morning toward Chestnut Hill. The Marquis had received word of our movement, and pulled back across the Schuylkill as quickly as possible. The English Light Dragoons, which had marched with the first corps, fell on the enemy rear, and took some prisoners. The entire army

Jaeger Corps Journal

marched out because the commanding general wanted to cut Lafayette off from the main army, and attack General Washington in his camp. As this did not succeed, toward evening the army marched back to Philadelphia.

May 24 - Sir William Howe went on board the warship *Europa* to return to England, and Sir Henry Clinton now commands as general-in-chief.

May 25 - The army's heavy baggage was taken on board ship.

May 26 - All wives, sick invalids, etc., also went aboard ship today, and the ships and the army are to be ready to move out at a moment's notice.

May 29 - 31 - The ships sailed from Philadelphia, and only a few vessels remain for use when the army moves out.

June 5 - The English commissioners arrived in Philadelphia to arrange a peace. All their efforts were in vain however, because the Americans are relying strongly on the French, and will accept no suggestions to the contrary.

June 16 - The army left Philadelphia, and crossed the Delaware to Jersey, at Cooper's Ferry.

June 18 - Today the rest of the troops left the city, and were transported across to Gloucester Point. The enemy army gave not the least indication of harassing our crossing, but remained completely quiet in camp. They were however, ready to march on the shortest

Jaeger Corps Journal

notice.

June 17 [sic] - Lieutenant General von Knyphausen set out marching toward Haddonfield with the following troops: Hessian Jaegers in the van, the Queen's Rangers, Hessian Grenadiers, 2nd Battalion of Jersey Volunteers, Maryland Loyalists, Volunteers of Ireland and Caldonia. The rest of the army remained at the river to load the baggage of the army and to get reorganized. Near Haddonfield, the Jaegers encountered the first enemy post, which fired and then pulled back.

June 18 [sic] - Major General [Alexander] Leslie was given command of a light corps, which is to be the army's advance guard, and which consists of the following troops: Jaegers, Queen's Rangers, a detachment of Jersey Volunteers, and the 7th, 23rd, and 63rd Regiments. The main army is to march in two columns. The Jaegers skirmished constantly with an enemy scouting party, which slowly fell back, giving resistance at every defile, woods, or bridge, and tore up every bridge, and caused whatever other harassment they could. Because of the many woods, the advance guard camped in a quarry.

June 19 - At four o'clock in the morning, the army marched in the same order as yesterday. The advance guard camped at Frishtown [Fostertown?] by the Balley [Belly?] Bridge, which the enemy had dismantled, and which had to be rebuilt by the engineers. Today a captain was killed by an enemy scouting party, and we lost one jaeger killed and several wounded.

June 20 - The march continued today to Mount Holly, where the army is to be reunited, and where we made camp. The enemy Major General [William] Maxwell and his brigade had lain in this place and retreated to Trenton. It was a secure post which could have been very easily and well defended, but their retreat was made so hurriedly that they did not even break up the bridge.

June 21 - Day of rest. The rest of the army joined with us here. The Jaeger Corps had to camp before the army, on the road to Trenton and in a woods. [Maximillian] Cornelis [of the Ansbach Jaegers] was detached with fifty jaegers to burn some ships, which lay in Hancocus Creek.

June 22 - This morning at three o'clock, the army marched in the following order: Jaegers, Queen's Rangers, Engineers, Light Infantry, two wagons of entrenching equipment, 16th Dragoons, Grenadiers, two 12-pounders, one howitzer, the Guards, 3rd Brigade, three battalions of the 4th Brigade, six pontoons, and the rest of the entrenching equipment, the baggage, 5th Brigade, [Richard] Hovedon's Provincials. A battalion of the brigade flanked the baggage on the left, and Allen's Corps was on the right.

Jaeger Corps Journal

Colonel Dyke's Corps marched in the middle of the baggage, and all the other troops not listed here, marched in the column under Lieutenant General von Knyphausen. The advance guard halted in Springfield and covered the left flank of the army as it passed the road leading off to Trenton, so it would not be disturbed by the enemy from Trenton. The advance guard then became the rear guard.

The enemy made camp at Black Horse. The Jaegers were posted on the left wing, on the Trenton Road.

23 June - The army marched in two columns today, the right wing under Lieutenant General von Knyp-, hausen, and the left wing under Lord Cornwallis. Leslie's Corps was the advance guard for the left column, and went to Bordentown to the drawbridge (a bridge over Crosswick Creek which could be lifted) which had been torn up. The corps camped there, the Jaegers in front, occupying the bridge. On the opposite side of the creek the enemy had thrown up rifle pits, which were however, not occupied. Toward evening a detachment of about fifty men entered these positions and fired at the Jaeger camp with small arms. These were followed by [Daniel] Morgan's Corps with two 6-pounders, which cannonaded the Jaegers. We remained quietly in our camp, and answered with our two 3-pounders. Our pickets however, continually fired their rifles, until nightfall brought an end to the

Jaeger Corps Journal

exchange. We had several wounded, and our powder cart was damaged by a cannonball. Later in the evening, we moved back behind a height so that we would not draw the enemy cannon fire again in the morning.

This morning, the right column encountered an enemy corps at Crosswick, which was engaged in dismantling the bridge at that place. A skirmish resulted, from which the enemy received considerable injury, and were then chased away.

June 24 - At three o'clock in the morning, Leslie's Corps marched to Crosswick, and took post so as to cover the left flank of the army, which was already marching on the Trenton side, and thereafter would become the rear guard. There were confirmed reports that the enemy had already crossed the Delaware near Trenton. During this afternoon, the Jaegers saw men from previously unseen units, and these troops harassed us greatly. The army camped this night near Englishtown. The Jaegers stood on the main road, in the middle of the army.

June 25 - The march today was as far as Upper Freehold. The Jaegers, in the rear guard, were severely harassed by the enemy, who pressed us vigorously. We laid an ambush which made them cautious.

June 26 - Today the army marched to Monmouth, where it camped on a very beautiful plain. The

Jaeger Corps Journal

Jaegers camped in a very pleasant grove of nut trees on the road to Trenton. Due to the unbearable heat, we lost three men. The march was very tiring, and as we were the last troops and constantly engaged with the enemy, and because of the exhausted and ruined wells, suffered severely from the shortage of water, many of the jaegers fell on the road, and were put on the officers' horses in order to be carried along with us, as we were not allowed any wagons. This happened frequently on the retreat across the Jerseys.

Today the enemy launched two very vigorous attacks on our rear in an effort to cut it off, but these were beaten back with losses. We laid an ambush into which a troop of cavalry fell, and several were shot.

June 27 - Day of rest. The enemy army had truly crossed the Delaware, and lay encamped near Grambury.

June 28 - The army was ordered to march in a column a certain distance to a place where Lieutenant General von Knyphausen was marching with the army's train and baggage. At this point, the Jaegers would become the rear guard, and to this end, joined the column at two o'clock in the morning at Monmouth, near the general's quarters, to which the 40th Regiment, under Lieutenant Colonel Musgrave, and the Jersey Volunteers also came. These preparations started the army in march, and as it took a long time to get the numerous wagons moving, it was

Jaeger Corps Journal

already six o'clock in the morning before all were under way. At this time, General Washington with his army marched up, and General Clinton awaited contact with only the left column, under Lord Cornwallis. The enemy, as soon as he had advanced a predetermined distance, formed in two lines, and General Clinton advanced against the enemy, and drove the first line completely back, and would have pursued it further if the second line had not been posted most advantageously on a height behind a swamp, which prevented him from doing so. Nevertheless, the English Grenadiers did make an effort to cross [the] morass, but got their cannon stuck, and were only able to retrieve them with the most strenuous effort. During this time, various attempts were made to capture the baggage, but these failed, and as a strong corps was reported marching against our train, which was stretched over as very long distance, the Jaeger Corps and the 40th Regiment were detached to provide cover. However, as the enemy had been beaten, that corps of his force was ordered back, and no engagement occurred here. General Clinton harassed the enemy throughout the day with artillery fire, and as his men were extremely fatigued, he did not desire to attack the enemy a second time, while they held such an advantageous position. However, he ordered a brigade from General von Knyphausen's column to join with his force in case the

Jaeger Corps Journal

enemy should launch an attack. As this did not happen, his men followed those of General von Knyphausen, which encamped below Middletown. The losses on the English side in this action amounted to 320 dead and wounded, and on the enemy side, to six hundred.

June 29 - The Stirn's Brigade, [Major General Johann Daniel von Stirm], was detached to Middletown early today, to occupy the heights in that region, and to deny them to the enemy. General Clinton joined forces with General von Knyphausen's column at ten o'clock this evening.

June 30 - The army marched at daybreak this morning to Middletown, and also encamped on the heights.

Jaeger Corps Journal

July 1 - The army departed this naturally secure post and occupied an advantageous position on the heights at Navesink. Today the baggage was brought to the bay at Sandy Hook in order to be embarked. We awaited in this position, formed in a crescent, an attack from the enemy, but no one appeared before our outposts except Morgan's Corps.

General [Charles] Lee had a falling out with General Washington concerning the action on the 28th, in which Lee was criticized for unnecessary retreating, and for not maintaining discipline in the first line.

July 2, 3, and 4 - The troops lay completely quiet while the baggage was transferred over to Sandy Hook.

July 5 - As the enemy army moved to Braunschweig, and from there toward the North River, in order to protect the Highlands, we did not expect further attack from it. Therefore, the King's army crossed over the bridge of ships to Sandy Hook, from whence they took ship to New York and Long Island and Staten Island. But their cavalry had to remain two days on Sandy Hook (a sandy bank on which a lighthouse for shipping stood), and were transferred to Long Island, where they camped eight days before rejoining the corps.

July 9 - Today the French fleet, consisting of twelve ships of the line, and three frigates, anchored at Sandy Hook. It had come from the Delaware, which

Jaeger Corps Journal

our fleet had left only a few days before. We can expect nothing except an attack on New York, for which reason, we hope soon to see Admiral [John] Byron, who was to have followed the French from England, and is supposed to have a decisive naval force with him. We have taken all possible defensive measures.

July 15 - General Washington crossed the North River, and camped at White Plains. The Jaeger Corps marched to a site in front of Kingsbridge, and camped on Spitting Devil. The enemy outpost stood at Valentine Hill and the Philipse's House, four miles from our posts.

July 18 - The enemy fleet sailed out to sea, without having taken any action. Reportedly, Washington has detached troops to Rhode Island.

The Jaeger Corps made a patrol to Philipse's House, and made contact with the enemy's most advanced outposts, which were very advantageously situated on the far side of a creek, on a very steep hill. After exchanging a few shots, Lieutenant Colonel von Wurmb pulled his corps back into camp.

July 26 - The news that Rhode Island is under siege, and that the French fleet sailed there, seems to be factual. Meantime, Lord [Richard] Howe has assembled all his warships, if not to attack the French under [Charles Hector] Comte d'Estaing, at least to annoy him until Admiral Byron arrives, which we anticipate will occur at any hour, as one of his ships has already arrived at Halifax. We are greatly concerned about Rhode Island, and doubt that the garrison there can withstand a siege. The defenses at Kingsbridge are to be improved, and new defenses erected, which keeps the army busy at this time. The English light troops are encamped in front of the redoubts on Hotham Heights, and skirmishes occur frequently with the enemy. The Jaeger Corps patrols from the heights at Spitting Devil to the enemy post at Philipse's House. NB - Spitting Devil is a continuation of the hills of Kingsbridge, from which it is cut off from York Island by the Harlem Creek, as far as Philipsburg. To the left flows the North River, and on the right, an arm of the Harlem Creek covers for some distance.

Aug. 3 - During the past night, a fire broke out in New York, which left seventy houses in ashes. Reportedly the fire was set.

Aug. 10 - Congress has found it necessary to detach a brigade against Colonel [John] Butler, who commands the Indians, and all the inhabitants who live along the area bordering the Indians, have had to flee to escape the depredations of the Indians.

Aug. 20 - According to certain information, the French fleet entered the harbor at Rhode Island on August 9, and then saw Lord Howe's fleet on August 10. They raised anchor to sail against Lord Howe.

Jaeger Corps Journal

Also, General [John] Sullivan has blockaded Newport, so General Clinton has detached four thousand men from the army, and has himself gone up the Sound to relieve Rhode Island.

Sept. 7 - Today General Clinton returned from Rhode Island, after the French had withdrawn, and the garrison was secure. He arrived there with four thousand men, unfortunately one day too late to engage General Sullivan on the island. As it could no longer be supported by the French fleet, Sullivan raised the siege on August 29 and was then closely pursued during his retreat. Lord Howe had kept the Comte d'Estaing occupied with his maneuvers, and both fleet had been scattered by a storm, so only a few engagements between individual ships occurred. The *Zele* a 74-gun ship, engaged the 50-gun *Iris*, and had to break off the battle. The 50-gun *Renown* engaged the 90-gun *Languedoc* for a considerable time , but in the end had to retire, because six other French ships were approaching. Another duel took place between the *Breston* and the *Tonant,* which was indecisive. Meanwhile, the French fleet reassembled and has sailed to Boston. Our fleet remains at Rhode Island until the four thousand-man force, which went with General Clinton, returns from Martha's Vineyard, where they had gone under command of Major General Gray, to get cattle for the fleet and the army. The inhabitants of that island, which lies in Buzzard's

Jaeger Corps Journal

Bay, were agreeable to the idea, and also surrendered up all their weapons on the previously agreed upon terms of not having their homes plundered.

Sept. 16 - This night two hundred jaegers, under Major von Prueschenck went to Philipse's House, and overran the picket there. The Queen's Rangers had taken another route in order to strike the enemy. Both detachments arrived at the same time, but the enemy had been alerted, and only two officers and 28 men were captured.

Sept. 18 - The enemy army is moving in order to draw back toward White Plains.

Sept. 20 - Major General Gray returned from Martha's Vineyard with the four thousand men.

Sept. 22 - The enemy army has been posted as follows: Headquarters at Peekskill; General [Horatio] Gates on the border of New England; a corps under General [Charles] Scott at Tarrytown, mans the outposts in the Newcastle district.

Sept. 23 - A part of the army marched today under Lieutenant General von Knyphausen to Philipse's House, and extended the camp from the North River to the Bronx River on the heights from Philipse's House to Valentine's House. The Jaegers are posted before the left wing on the North River. The other part of the army under General Clinton went into Jersey and camped near Newbridge.

Sept. 28 - This night, a detachment of the Light

Jaeger Corps Journal

Infantry attacked a regiment of enemy dragoons in the Jerseys and captured it. The unit was known as Lady Washington's Dragoons, and consisted of about one hundred men. The Queen's Rangers, who, to support the Light Infantry, had crossed the North River the previous night, returned and entered camp on the right wing, which during their absence, had been occupied by 120 jaegers (Captain Ewald).

Sept. 30 - A patrol of eighty foot jaegers, under Captain [Carl Moritz] von Donop, and Lieutenant Mertz, with twelve cavalrymen, went to Dobb's Ferry early this morning to cover the foragers. A detachment under Major [Henry] Lee ambushed them, and cut off the cavalry and the most advanced infantry, consisting of Lieutenant [Alexander Wilhelm] Bickell, and twenty men of the main corps. Lieutenant Mertz tried to fight his way through with the cavalry, but was unable to do so, as he was surrounded by both mounted and dismounted enemy, and had to surrender after he was wounded, and three of his men were killed. The infantry lost only five men taken prisoner and two wounded, as they were able to retreat through the woods. The enemy was too strong for the captain to accomplish anything, and so he remained standing on the other side of the defile, and as Lieutenant Mertz had been captured, withdrew. The entire corps moved out upon hearing of the attack, but arrived too late, as the enemy had already retired.

Jaeger Corps Journal

Oct. 1 - The Jaeger Corps, Queen's Rangers, Legion, and Lieutenant Colonel [Andreas] Emmerich's Corps, all under the command of Lieutenant Colonel von Wurmb, marched this night; the first along the Sawmill River Road, and the English over Tuckahoe, to attack an enemy corps lying near Hammond's House. Unfortunately, however, the Jaegers ran into a picket about four o'clock in the morning, which no one knew about. The picket fired and advanced upon our force, which at once pulled back. Our troops returned the same evening, very tired from the long march.

Oct. 3 - This morning at ten o'clock an enemy patrol alerted the Grenadier outposts on Sawmill Road, and after exchanging a few shots, hurriedly retired.

Oct. 4 - Reports are that the enemy headquarters is at Quakerhill, two brigades are at North Berry, and General Scott with the Flying Corps and cavalry is at Bedford. These dispositions make it clear that Washington does not intend to attack New York, although some had expected him to do so.

Oct. 10 - Today the army marched back to its previous camp at Kingsbridge, and the Light Infantry once again returned to Spitting Devil and Hotham Heights.

Oct. 13 - Today an enemy cavalry patrol alarmed the Jaeger Corps, captured an outpost, and then

Jaeger Corps Journal

quickly withdrew.

Oct. 14 - The English fleet made preparations to sail to the West Indies. Four thousand English under Major General Grant were embarked.

Nov. 6 - Another expeditions of about 2,500 men, consisting of [Oliver] Delancey's Corps, York Volunteers, and the [Hessian] Wissembach and Woellworth Regiments were embarked today, but the destination remains secret.

Nov. 13 - We received news today that the enemy army has entered winter quarters, and that the headquarters is at Chatham in Jersey.

Nov. 16 - The royal army entered winter quarters on York Island and Staten Island. The Jaegers were at Flushing on Long Island, the officers in houses, but the men had to build huts, for which purpose nails and tools were delivered.

Nov. 29 - Upon receipt of news that the prisoners from Burgoyne's army were to be transported from New England to Virginia, and would cross the North River at Kings's Ferry, the British Grenadiers, Light Infantry, and the Mirbach Regiment marched to Tarrytown, but arrived too late; the men being transferred having crossed the North River ten hours previously. The reason these troops are being sent to Virginia is supposedly because the New Englanders refuse to continue giving them provisions.

So ends the campaign for the year 1778. Both

Jaeger Corps Journal

armies remained in their winter quarters, nothing being undertaken by either side, and we directed our attention and our hopes to the operations in the West Indies.

Jaeger Corps Journal

1779

Jan. 1 - As the provisions for the army were exhausted, and the long awaited fleet from Cork had not yet arrived, rations became scarce. Therefore, one half was issued as oatmeal instead of bread, and from the eighth to the twentieth, the army received zwieback made from oatmeal.

Jan. 18 - The provisions fleet from Cork arrived today.

Feb. 1 - Today we received the good news that the royal fleet commanded by Admiral [James] Barrington had taken the West Indies island of St. Lucia from the French.

The English fleet departed from Barbados on December 12, 1778, and anchored in Grand Cul de Sac. Early on the thirteenth, the troops landed while it was still dark, and took possession of the island early on the fourteenth, without encountering resistance. The same afternoon, the French fleet, under Monsieur d'Estaing, arrived and attacked the English lying in the bay. He remained at too great a distance to do any serious damage, and toward evening, anchored some distance away. On the sixteenth, the French were moving constantly, and landed their troops. On the eighteenth they attacked the English on land, but were driven back by Major [William] Meadows, although they twice stormed the English lines. On the 24th, d'Estaing departed, after re-embarking the land troops, which had accomplished nothing, and sailed from the island to Port Royal.

Feb. 13 - We also received the good news from Colonel [Archibald] Campbell that he had occupied Georgia, with the troops which had sailed from New York on November 6, and defeated the enemy troops under General [Robert] Howe near Savannah. Colonel Campbell, after much bad weather, arrived at Tybee Island on December 23, and went up the Savannah River as far as Gerardot's Plantation, which was the first practical landing place. Here the troops were landed on the 27th. Fifty rebels posted there opened fire, but were driven off, and the landing site secured. Major General Howe, commanding the Americans, marched to the east end of the city of Savannah, where he was immediately attacked by Colonel Campbell, and forced to flee. Howe's force of four thousand men retreated so quickly through the woods that only a few men were taken prisoner.

May 1 - The 42nd Regiment, the [Hessian] Prince Charles Regiment, [Francis] Lord Rawdon's Corps, and the grenadier company of the Guards were embarked under Brigadier General [Edward] Mathews to destroy enemy magazines and ships along the coast of Virginia, and primarily in Chesapeake Bay.

May 29 - The army was ordered to reassemble and encamp on the opposite side from Kingsbridge. The corps and regiments which had been in cantonments

Jaeger Corps Journal

moved out at daybreak, passed Kingsbridge at seven o'clock in the morning, and marched in the following order: to Philipse's House: the mounted jaegers (NB: these marched from Flushing over Brooklyn, where they crossed the East River), the Hessian Grenadiers and the Bose Regiment. To Williamsbridge: Queen's Rangers, Legion, 7th and 63rd Regiments. To Valentine's Hill: [Patrick] Ferguson's Corps, Light Infantry, 17th Dragoons, and Robinson's Corps. To Mile Square: Emmerich's Corps, 17th, 23rd, 33rd, and 64th Regiments. The dismounted Jaegers marched from Flushing to Whitestone, crossed the East River, and marched over Westchester to Philipse's House. The English Grenadiers marched at the same time from Jamaica, along the same route to Whitestone, crossing the river after the Jaegers, and then camped at Eastchester.

Defensive Dispositions

Jaegers			Ferguson				Legion	Emmerich			Rangers	
A	B	C	D	64	33	23	17	E	F	G	63	7 H

A-Linsingen B-Minnigerode C-Lengerke D-Bose E-Robinson F-17th Dragoons G-Light Infantry H-English Grenadiers

The right wing stretched from Eastchester to the Bronx River, the center from the Bronx River to the Sawmill, and the left wing from there to the North

Jaeger Corps Journal

River. Major General Vaughan commanded the English troops, Major General [Henrich Julius] von Kospoth, the Hessians, and Major General [Sir William] Erskine, the army's various light troops.

May 30 - At one o'clock this afternoon, Brigadier General Mathew returned from Virginia with his detachment, and lay at anchor near Philipse's House. He left Portsmouth six days ago, having captured and burned many ships, and seized a large amount of booty.

The following troops were ordered to embark at once near Philipse's House: The English and Hessian Grenadiers, the legionaires-dismounted, Robinson's Corps, Light Infantry, 17th, 63rd, and 64th Regiments, and three hundred jaegers, under Major von Prueschenck. The embarkation was completed about ten o'clock.

May 31 - At two o'clock this morning, the troops aboard ship moved up the North River, and at eleven o'clock, anchored at Fertride Hook (also known as Tallerspoint [Tellar's Point]. One hundred jaegers, the 17th, 63rd, and 64th Regiments, as well as Robinson's Corps, at once debarked on the west bank at Stony Point, where a detachment of the enemy had begun, but not yet completed, some defensive works, which they left immediately. Major General [James] Pattison who commanded this detachment, occupied these works and set up a battery at once, while Major

Jaeger Corps Journal

General Vaughan landed the rest of the troops on the east bank at Verplanck's Point, where the enemy had built Fort Lafayette, and occupied it with a detachment. This was blockaded by General Vaughan. Major General Erskine, who commanded the rest of the army at Philipse's House, marched out toward ten o'clock in the morning to the heights at Dobb's Ferry, where he took post with the right wing, protected by the heights of the Sawmill, and the left by the North River.

Jaegers			Rangers	
Emmerich	Bose	17th Dragoons	23rd	7th

June 1 - Major General Pattison opened fire on Fort Lafayette from Stony Point at daybreak this morning, with a battery containing one 12-pounder and a howitzer, with such good effect that the enemy captain commanding therein, plus four subalterns and seventy men, surrendered about ten o'clock. The fort was a regular rectangle with double palisades and a moat.

General Erskine sent out a patrol to the other side of White Plains today to reconnoiter the enemy, and to observe the movements of General Gates, who was at Providence, but Erskine was unable to obtain definite information, nor to learn anything about the enemy.

June 3 - On reports that the enemy had assembled

Jaeger Corps Journal

a number of cattle on the Croton River, in order to provision his army and to prevent our seizing them, General Erskine marched at eleven o'clock with the Cavalry, Jaegers, Rangers, the 23rd Regiment and two hundred men of the Bose Regiment, leaving all baggage behind, to Sing Sing, where the 23rd Regiment and a detachment of the Bose Regiment were posted on the road to White Plains. The remaining troops marched off on the North Castle Road. The Cavalry and the Rangers seized the cattle and eighteen men watching them, and drove the cattle back to the camp at Dobb's Ferry, for use by the royal hospital. The Jaegers served as a rear guard on the return march, which took place at night, but they were not followed.

June 4 - The army celebrated the King's birthday today by marching out and firing a feu de joie.

June 5 - The 42nd Regiment, Prince Charles Regiment, and Lord Rawdon's Corps returned from Stony Point today, and went into the army's former camp at Philipse's House. The corps of Major General Erskine also marched there from Dobb's Ferry.

June 6 - General Clinton came from Stony Point today, scouted the lines near Philipse's House, and then set up his quarters in Philipsburg.

June 7 - According to information received, the enemy army has finally moved from the Jerseys toward West Point, in order to defend Fort Defiance

Jaeger Corps Journal

and the Highlands.

June 8 - Major General Erskine conducted a patrol with the Cavalry today to White Plains. He met some militia at North Castle. Nine were captured, some were cut down, and a number of cattle were seized. The house of the enemy colonel, [Evan] Thomas, with all the furniture therein, was burned during this raid, because as a prisoner of war, he had broken his parole by commanding a militia regiment, prior to his being exchanged.

June 11 - As the new construction at Stony Point is nearing completion, cannon were sent up the North River today for installation there.

June 15 - The Jaeger Corps and the Rangers made a patrol today, but the enemy came no further than the Croton Bridge, to which point he had sent his patrol.

June 17 - A sloop which arrived from Georgia yesterday evening, brought the news that Major General [Augustine] Prevost had advanced from Savannah to the vicinity of Charleston, that on May 8 he had occupied Sullivan's Island and captured Fort Johnson, and further, that he had made preparations to put Charleston under siege.

June 18 - General Washington is encamped at Smith's Gloves, and reportedly has only a very weak army. General Gates is still in Providence with the New Englanders, as a covering force for the borders of New England.

Jaeger Corps Journal

June 19 - Instead of Major General Erskine, who is returning to England, the command will now be held by Major General Mathew, whose troops are camped at Philipsburg.

June 24 - Lieutenant Colonel von Wurmb received the assignment of reconnoitering the enemy's outposts with the light troops, and where possible, to attack in order to get information about their army. Therefore, the Queen's Rangers had to march to Pontsbridge during the past night, while the Legion went off to the right at the same time, to cut an enemy corps at Crambond off from the pass leading to Bedford. The enemy had however, already pulled back the day before, leaving a small outpost of forty men somewhat further back. This post was captured by the Rangers. The Jaeger Corps marched to Hortam's [Hotham?] Heights, and the 17th Dragoon Regiment marched to the right over David's Hill, at White Plains (the same place on which the enemy camp stood in 1776 when General Howe attacked) to the designated rendezvous. Here the Jaegers and the 17th Dragoons joined together at about one o'clock in the afternoon, without either force having encountered any enemy. An enemy cavalry patrol was seen at four o'clock. Our cavalry tried, unsuccessfully, to make contact. The next morning the Rangers and the Legion joined with the above troops on David's Hill, and as all the enemy outposts had been pulled back, Lieutenant Colonel

Jaeger Corps Journal

von Wurmb was left standing here, waiting for the return of scouts which had been sent out, in order to get some information. He then marched on

June 26 - back to the camp at Philipse's House.

June 27 - The construction at Stony Point and Verplanck's Point is completed and now consists of the following: Stony Point: Lieutenant Colonel [Henry] Johnston, forty cannon and one hundred artillerymen, 17th and 33rd Regiments, and Ferguson's Corps. Verplanck's Point: Lieutenant Colonel [James] Webster, twenty cannon and forty artillerymen, 63rd Regiment, Robinson's Corps, and two companies of grenadiers.

The positions cover King's Ferry, the main road from Boston, and all of New England to Philadelphia and the southern provinces, which greatly handicaps the enemy. The rest of the troops embarked today in order to join the army at Philipse's House.

June 28 - The troops which had come from Stony Point entered the camp in the line of the army.

June 29 - Lieutenant Colonel Emmerich, during the past night, surprised a small picket on Bryant's Bridge, killing eleven men and capturing the rest.

July 1 - A party from Staten Island marched during the past night to Woodbridge in the Jerseys, attacked a small enemy post there, and captured one officer and twelve dragoons.

July 2 - The Cavalry of the Jaeger Corps, the

Jaeger Corps Journal

Legion, and the Rangers marched today out of the camp at Philipse's House (under Colonel Banastree Tarleton), in order to attack an enemy cavalry detachment at Poundreach. At three o'clock in the morning of July 3, they encountered an enemy outpost. Because of a lack of clarity in the road markers, they had stumbled into the road leading to the enemy camp, which gave the enemy time to retire, although with the loss of many horses, saddles, and equipment. A standard, one officer, and 22 men fell into our hands. During the return march, the Cavalry was harassed by the militia, which did only limited damage.

July 3 - During the preceding night, the 7th and 23rd Regiments, as well as forty jaegers (under Lieutenant Bickell) went to Frog's Neck to unite there with the 54th Regiment, Landgraf Regiment, and Fanning's Corps, which arrived yesterday from Rhode Island, and are to undertake an expedition, under Major General [William] Tryon, against the New England coast.

July 4 - The troops under Major General Tryon sailed up the Sound.

July 5 - The English and Hessian Grenadiers, the Light Infantry, 17th Dragoons, the Legion, and the Rangers received orders to be ready to march.

July 7 - This morning the above mentioned troops under General Vaughan were put in motion, marched to Mamaroneck and camped there, between Kingsbridge and this place, in order to protect the people making hay.

July 8 - News reports are to the effect that the enemy Major General Sullivan, with his subordinate brigadiers, [George] Clinton, Maxwell, [Enoch] Poor, Hand, and [James] Potter, arrived at Wyoming on the Susquehanna on June 23, in order to drive off the Indian partisans, Butler and [Joseph] Brant.

From Savannah, we hear that General Prevost, with his army, appeared before Charleston on the evening of May 11, which caused the enemy to set fire to the suburbs. On May 12, he called upon the city to surrender, and gave it four hours to consider the demand. The city officials entered negotiations, knowing that General [Benjamin] Lincoln was marching to protect the city, and this saved them, because General Prevost did not want to storm the city with the enemy approaching. Instead, he pulled back to Farnes Island.

July 14 - Major General Tryon with the detachment under his command, which sailed from Frog's Neck on July 4, issued a proclamation to the inhabitants of New England, to lay down their arms, and promised to protect them, if they would remain peacefully in their homes. Thereafter, on July 5, he landed at New Haven in order to determine the attitude of the inhabitants. However, he found they

Jaeger Corps Journal

had abandoned the city, and the militia had occupied a defensive position called Black Rock. He did not wish to attack this position, but drove a part of the enemy out of the city, where they had taken post, burned all the public buildings and magazines, and returned to his ships the next morning. On the sixth, he sailed to Fanfield [Fairfield?], burned the city, as the inhabitants had all taken up arms, reembarked and sailed to Huntington Bay. He sailed from there, on the eleventh, to Norwalk, laid this place in ashes also, and then returned to Whitestone on the twelfth. The forty jaegers, who were engaged with the militia most of the time, lost two killed, four wounded, and three made prisoners.

July 16 - During the past night, about two o'clock, we heard a short cannonade at Stony Point, which we believed meant an outpost there was being attacked. In that we were not mistaken, and heard to our amazement, the next day, that the enemy had attacked and captured Stony Point.

July 17 - The brigade of Major General [Thomas] Sterling was embarked on the North River very early this morning in order to recapture Stony Point, but because of contrary winds, could not sail.. General Vaughan, who was posted at Mamaroneck to protect the hay-makers, returned today to camp by Philipse's House. Major General Tryon with his detachment did the same. Thereafter, the Rangers, Legion, and the

Jaeger Corps Journal

17th Dragoons marched to Crambond in order to support Verplanck's Point, where Lieutenant Colonel Webster commanded, because an enemy attack was expected following the loss of Stony Point.

July 18 - The army marched to Dobb's Ferry and occupied that positions, where a part of the army had been on May 31, during the first capture of Stony Point, in order, once again, to support the operations against Stony Point. Meanwhile, several frigates had already sailed up the river, and before Major General Sterling could arrive, the enemy abandoned the post. However, he had taken with him all the artillery except for a few heavy pieces. Still, a sloop with eleven cannon on board, was captured from him because the sloop, due to the ebbtide, had grounded.

July 19 - Sterling's Brigade reoccupied Stony Point, and the defenses, which because of the enemy's short period of occupation, could not be fully destroyed, were again improved. The enemy General Wayne made the following report about this affair to General Washington:

He marched with twelve hundred men, special troops, from Sandy Beach, at noon on July 15, and arrived that evening at eight o'clock at Mr. Springfield's plantation, a mile and a half from the fort. Here, the troops were halted and formed up until the defenses could be reconnoitered. At eleven-thirty the troops advanced. On the right wing, one hundred fifty

Jaeger Corps Journal

volunteers under Colonel Fleury formed the advance guard, of which one officer and twenty men with axes cleared a path through the palisades ahead of the main advance. On the left wing, there was also a detachment of one hundred volunteers under Major Stewart, with one officer and twenty men serving as engineers. These advance detachments had not loaded their weapons. At twelve-thirty the attack began. The fort was completely surrounded, overrun, and surrendered with a minimal loss of life on the enemy side, after a short fight.

We received news from South Carolina that General Lincoln, on June 20, had attacked Colonel [John] Maidland, who was posted on James Island with the 71st Regiment and Truembach Regiment. However, the bravery of these troops enabled them to repel Lincoln's attack. Lincoln made his attack just at that time, when many soldiers were absent unloading provisions, and attacked with great ferocity.

July 20 - The Rangers, Legion, and 17th Dragoons returned today from Verplanck's Point and camped on the right wing of the army.

July 21 - The Jaeger Corps marched from the left to the right wing of the army, in order to cover the right flank, and took post in a woods at Tuckahoe.

We received news today that Lord Cornwallis had arrived in New York from England in the frigate *Greyhound*, whereupon the army on July 22 - marched

Jaeger Corps Journal

back to the previous camp at Philipse's House.

July 30 - Lieutenant Colonel von Wurmb made a patrol today to Tarrytown with the mounted Jaegers, and one hundred eighty foot Jaegers. The Cavalry encountered an enemy force of sixty horses, which fled, and during the pursuit, lost only one man. Four men from Emmerich's Dragoons were recaptured from the enemy, having been captured this morning during a skirmish.

July 31 - Early today the army marched back to Kingsbridge. The regiments and corps occupied the emplacements at this place, which they had occupied before. The Jaeger Corps was again on Spitting Devil.

Aug. 1 - An English captain from a transport ship, who with 38 sailors, had deserted from prisoner of war status, arrived in New York in a sloop from Boston, and brought the news that the Bostonains had outfitted a fleet in order to go to Penobscot to capture the English post, which had recently been established under Brigadier General McLain, at that place, for the purpose of protecting the woodsmen cutting timbers for building ships. Therefore, Commodore George Collier sailed with the *Raisonable* and the frigates *Greyhound, Blonde, Virginia, Galathea, Camilla*, and the sloop *Otter,* to disrupt the enemy's plans.

N.B. The favorable outcome of this expedition is under September 9.

Aug. 5 - An enemy cavalry patrol engaged the

outpost at Hotham Heights and captured some loyalists [referred to in the journal as refugees] in the neighborhood of the Legion. The Legion, Rangers, and also the Jaegers set out in pursuit, and a part of the Legion made contact the other side of New Rochelle. The enemy had been joined by forty infantrymen, who fired on the Legion, and then scattered, having killed two men and wounded seven. The Rangers and Jaegers arrived too late.

Aug. 6 - The defenses at Laurel Hill are being hastily improved.

Aug 10 - We received news that Grenada and St. Vincent had been captured from the French, and that on July 6, an indecisive engagement had taken place at sea, between Admiral Byron and d'Estaing.

Aug. 18 - Thirty ships arrived at New York from Georgia, bringing the news that the royal troops were being quartered during the summer heat, part at Beaufort, and a part at Savannah.

Aug. 19 - During the past night the enemy Major Lee, with four hundred men, stormed Paulus Hook. He passed the moat in front of the abitis, the abitis itself, and entered the position before the Englanders were aware, and captured them. A Hessian non-commissioned officer with fifteen men, who had the picket in a blockhouse, ran out in order to see what was happening. He and ten men were captured. Captain [Henrich Sebastian von] Schallern however,

Jaeger Corps Journal

with one officer and 25 men, threw themselves into a small redoubt, and began firing at the enemy. Although called upon to surrender, he held his post. The enemy, therefore, retreated with his prisoners, (one hundred men), after having set fire to several barracks. A battalion of light infantry and Buskirk's Provincials, which were shipped over from New York, pursued the enemy as far as Newbridge, but could not overtake them.

Aug. 26 - Vice Admiral [Marriot] Arbuthnot sailed into New York from England with the first division of the merchant fleet. He had the newly raised 80th and 81st Regiments, as well as English recruits on board.

Sept. 2 - By the July packet, which left Falmouth on July 7, we learned that England has found it necessary to declare war against Spain, and this happened today in New York when Governor Tyron conducted the usual formalities.

Sept. 8 - The 40th Regiment and Lossberg and Knyphausen Regiments embarked in order to sail to Canada.

Jaeger Corps Journal

Sept. 9 - Sir George Collier's expedition against the New England fleet has had rather good consequences. Sir George sailed on August 2 with his squadron from Sandy Hook, and reached the Penobscot River early on the fourteenth. The enemy squadron had already been blockading Brigadier General McLain for three weeks, and the last thing they expected to see was the English fleet. Initially it appeared as if they would defend themselves. Instead however, they sailed up the river after taking on board the soldiers who had been conducting the blockade on land. On the approach of the English ships, they set fire to their ships, and the troops retreated into the woods. The sloop *Hunter,* of eighteen cannon, and *Hampton* of twenty cannon, fell into English hands before they could be set on fire. The remaining ships which burned, were fourteen ships, armed with 32 to 16 cannon, as well as 24 transport ships, so that not a single ship escaped. Sir George had the good fortune to capture the brig *Nancy,* of sixteen cannon and *Rover,* of ten cannon, at sea, while they were cruising before their fleet, and therefore enabled the complete surprise of the squadron. The enemy had to make their return trip to Boston through the forest, which for the most part, is uninhabited and a wilderness.

Sept. 10 - Today the destruction of the redoubts on Hotham Heights began, as the new line at Laurel Hill is nearly completed. In this manner, in the future, the

Jaeger Corps Journal

royal line will be reduced to being only on York Island, and will be covered by the Harlem Creek, enabling it to be more easily defended, and with fewer people.

Sept. 13 - Colonel Tarleton with the Cavalry, the Legion, and twenty mounted jaegers, marched from here this evening to attack an enemy cavalry detachment at Northcastle. He arrived there early the next morning, and found that the enemy had already retreated. He captured several prisoners from a picket, the men of which had become scattered. During his return march, he was followed by the cavalry of Lieutenant White, and the militia, and lost eight men.

Sept. 16 - The 64th Regiment left its post at Verplanck's Point and went to New York.

The following regiments received orders to be prepared to embark, and supposedly to sail to the southward: the Grenadiers, two hundred jaegers, the Light Infantry, the Rangers, 7th, 23rd, 37th, 54th, and 57th Regiments, as well as Fanning's Corps. Also, an express boat brought the news from General [Sir John] Dalling at Jamaica, that the French threatened to attack his island, and there were not enough troops for its defense.

Sept. 17 - Lord Cornwallis was embarked with the 7th, 23rd, 33rd, and 57th Regiments, Queen's Rangers, and Irish Volunteers in order to go to Jamaica.

Sept 18 - All posts the other side of Kingsbridge

were withdrawn today. Only the Jaeger Corps remained standing completely alone, in order to occupy the Spitting Devil. We were thus much exposed, and lay completely cut off from the army. Most of the time during the night we were kept under arms.

Sept. 19 - The Legion marched today to Oyster Bay on Long Island, in order to protect that island against the frequent plundering from the New Englanders, who cross the Sound.

Sept. 20 - The 64th Regiment entered camp behind the Jaeger Corps in order to support them, should the need arise.

Sept. 21 - Commodore Hammond, with the second division of the English merchant fleet, arrived at New York. He had the Hessian recruits on board.

Sept. 23 - The recruits were landed and sent to their designated regiments. The Jaeger Corps received two officers and 230 men.

Sept. 24 - Lord Cornwallis went to sea today.

Sept. 28 - A Spanish ship was captured by an English privateer, and in the log book it was found that the French fleet had been seen on August 31 on the Grand Banks, and on a westerly course.

This was the reason that Lord Cornwallis had been called back, and preparations made for the defense of New York, because Jamaica was therefore out of danger, and apparently New York must be the destination of the fleet. Lord Cornwallis returned therefore on

Sept. 29 - to Sandy Hook, whereupon the troops debarked and were placed for the protection of The Narrows and the landing places at Denyse's House.

Sept. 30 - A detachment of one hundred jaegers under Captain [Friedrich A.J.] von Wangenheim marched to Laurel Hill to take post in the camp evacuated by the Bose Regiment, which was ordered to New York.

Jaeger Corps Journal

Oct. 3 - A patrol from the Jaeger Corps encountered an enemy patrol this morning at Eastchester, and captured an officer and the trumpeter.

Oct. 4 - Of the troops, which on September 8 had sailed to Canada, a single ship returned, with the sad news that they had been scattered by a storm and some of them had been destroyed (which no one yet knows for certain). Further reports indicate that the sunken ship had a part of the Lossberg Regiment on board, and another, on which were Major [Johann Friedrich Georg] von Stein, with part of the Knyphausen Regiment, was captured by the enemy after having lost its mast and become a complete wreck, and that the troops had been saved.

News has been received that the enemy has occupied the Thunder Barracks (a height not far from Stony Point), and the brigade of Major General Howe has moved forward to Newcastle.

Oct 15 - The French fleet was seen on September 6 near Charleston, but it then turned immediately out to sea. Admiral Byron, because he is going to England, turned over command of the fleet to Admiral [Peter] Parker. At this time, as the French have sailed for the West Indies, it is assumed that they have gone to Jamaica.

Oct. 20 - The French fleet appeared off Tybee, and the troops on board were landed. They joined with the enemy army under General Lincoln, and immediately marched to Savannah in order to besiege General Prevost, while the fleet blockaded him by sea. The English warship *Experiment,* as well as another one, had already been captured, and as Savannah had only a small force, and as part of the English in Beaufort under Colonel Maidland could not join General Prevost, we are greatly concerned about the general's future. At this time, there is not the least assistance which can be given to him from here, because we have no fleet of warships here.

General Washington ordered his heavy artillery to West Point, and has called up four thousand militiamen, in case the French fleet should be able to cooperate against this army. General Sullivan, who has been detached against the Indians, has also returned, and has noticeably strengthened the enemy army.

The defensive works at New York are being worked on vigorously so that the army can defend itself, should the French attack with their fleet.

Oct.21 - Stony Point was abandoned this evening and the garrison returned to New York.

Oct 26 - The troops from Rhode Island arrived at New York and no troops are now stationed there.

The news from England says that the French and Spanish fleets have united, greatly outnumbering the English ships, and blockaded Plymouth, from August

Jaeger Corps Journal

20 to 24, but did not attack the port.

Nov. 6 - An enemy detachment of five hundred horses under Colonel White caused the Jaeger Corps to be alerted this morning, but engaged in no further action.

Nov. 7 - The army moved into designated winter quarters on York, Long, and Staten Island. The Jaeger Corps is to be cantoned in huts, which they must build for themselves on Laurel Hill. The enemy army still remains in the field awaiting the French fleet.

Nov.19 - Against all expectations, today we received the pleasant news that the siege of Savannah had been lifted, and the French have again returned to the West Indies.

General Prevost did his utmost to defend the city of Savannah, and if possible to hold it. Therefore, he had Major [James] Moncrief construct new defenses, which enabled him to defend his position against the enemy attacks. Colonel Maidland had also worked his way through impassable morasses and swamps, and arrived with his detachment, completely unexpected, in Savannah. Comte d'Estaing began a regular siege operation, and called upon the general a number of times to surrender to the weapons of the French king, but the general paid no heed, even though the city was completely surrounded. D'Estaing finally became restless, knowing the English fleet was in the West Indies. He no longer desired to wait for the extensive

Jaeger Corps Journal

and slow construction of the approaches, but stormed the defenses on November 11, at daybreak. However, he was beaten back. He was wounded and [Count Casimir] Pulaski, the second in command of the rebel generals, was killed. Thereupon, the enemy pulled back, re-embarking his artillery, and after several days, completely raised the siege. D'Estaing sailed to the West Indies, and General Lincoln marched with the rebels to Charleston.

The valiant Colonel Maidland had so weakened himself on the fatiguing march, that a few days after his arrival in Savannah, he contracted a fever and died. The royal losses were not very great.

Nov. 21 - The army marched out this evening and fired a feu de joie for the failure of the French siege of Savannah.

General Washington has quartered his army at Morristown.

Dec 19 - General Clinton now saw himself in a condition to continue the operations in the southern provinces, and to this end, the following troops were embarked today: English Grenadiers, Light Infantry, 7th, 23rd, 33rd, 42nd, 63rd, and 64th Regiments, 250 jaegers (under Major von Wurmb), the Hessian Grenadier Regiment Huyne, a detachment of chasseurs, one battalion of the 71st Regiment, Ferguson's Corps, the Legion, and the New York Volunteers.

Jaeger Corps Journal

Dec. 24 - The above troops sailed to Sandy Hook in eighty ships, under the cover of five ships of the line and five frigates. Lieutenant General von Knyphausen now commands New York and its attached posts.

Jaeger Corps Journal

1780

Jan. 15 - The continuing cold since Christmas Day has so covered the rivers with ice, that one can walk and ride across them. Therefore, General Washington considered this as an ideal time to undertake some action against the troops remaining here, and to take advantage of all the opportunities which this occasion offered. His first thought turned on the garrison on Staten Island. This island had been robbed of its natural defensive strength by the rivers freezing. The garrison was not strong, and appeared to be in great danger, especially as it could not be supported from New York, because the ice was not yet solid, and there was no way to make a crossing. General Washington had noted all this and detached General Stirling, with 3,500 men in sleds, which had been gathered at Morristown, and carried the men across the snow to Bergen, in order to attack the garrison. But the English General Stirling, who commanded on Staten Island, received reports of the enemy advance and was prepared to receive them. Not withstanding, the rebels crossed the ice during the night of Jan. 16, 1780 - near Decker's Ferry, and established outposts on Brusky Heights, cutting off the Queen's Rangers at Richmond, and the troops at the Flagstaff, from those in the headquarters' defenses at Cole's Ferry. General von Knyphausen ordered a

Jaeger Corps Journal

number of flat boats to be gathered at The Narrows, where because of the strong current, there was still some open water, and toward evening he ordered the 80th Regiment into the boats in order to try, if at all possible, to cross over during the next ebb tide.

The enemy did not want to risk storming these defenses from which all the snow had been removed. The cold was too great to tolerate for an extended period, and the fear that the embarked troops might surprise them, caused the enemy to pull back across the ice on the night of the seventeenth. A troop of English provincial dragoons attacked his rear guard, and many of the enemy suffered from frozen hands, feet, and ears.

Jan. 18 - An enemy party of 140 men overran a provincial outpost at Morrisiana during the night, and captured two of the outpost's staff officers. They set fire to the house and retreated. The loyalists regrouped, the captured major escaped, and at the head of the provincials, followed the enemy, catching up with them at New Rochelle, where twenty of the enemy were killed and 37 made prisoners.

Jan. 21 - The North and East Rivers are so completely covered with ice that cannon can be transported across them. It is now possible to cross to Staten Island (thirteen miles) with a wagon. New York therefore, is like a part of the mainland and is open to an enemy attack. Lieutenant General von Knyphausen

Jaeger Corps Journal

has taken all possible precautions to prevent such an occurrence. The Jaeger Corps was dressed every night, and constantly sent patrols along the North River, even though a chain of occupied defensive positions were already in existence there.

Jan. 22 - Tonight a party went from Staten Island to Elizabethtown, attacked the garrison there, captured a number of officers and 72 privates, and set the barracks on fire. Another party attacked an enemy picket at Newark and captured the personnel.

Feb. 3 - Colonel Norton with the Guards, and the mounted jaegers under Lieutenant Mertz, and one non-commissioned officer and fifteen foot jaegers marched from here during the past night in order to attack an enemy outpost at Young's House. They arrived there this morning at seven o'clock, and attacked the enemy, who defended his position from the house, and from behind a stonewall. After the house was set afire, the enemy surrendered. Five officers and 93 privates were made prisoners, and forty killed. Our losses were three English soldiers and one mounted jaeger killed, and twenty English and two jaegers wounded.

Mar. 22 - The warship *Russel* arrived at New York today. It came from the bar at Charleston, and brought the report that the fleet, under Sir Henry Clinton, after a 36 day voyage, during which it suffered many hardships, had arrived at Tybee Island, and left there

Jaeger Corps Journal

February 7, and landed the army on Johns Island, on February 9. General Clinton on March 1, occupied James Island and sent General Patterson, with a corps from Savannah, over Augusta to reunited with him again near Charleston, which place was to be put under siege, as the enemy army was there under General Lincoln. Several ships of the fleet are still missing, among others the *Anna*, on which a detachment of jaegers are said to be.

The designated troops were alerted to be ready to move into the field on short notice, and the 42nd Regiment, Ditfurth Regiment, and the Irish Volunteers were embarked near Charleston.

Apr. 5 - The brigatine *Speedwell,* in seven weeks from Lisbon, brought the news that Admiral [Sir George] Rodney, who had sailed from Portsmouth on December 26, 1779, with 21 ships of the line, in order to relieve Gibralter, and then proceed to the West Indies, fell in with a Spanish merchant fleet, escorted by a 64-gunship and four frigates near Cape Finisterrne on January 8, and then on the 16th, not far from Cadiz, with a squadron of eleven ships of the line, which they engaged. The admiral's ship carrying Admiral Don Juan de Languara was badly damaged, and four other ships of the line were captured. The action occurred during a strong wind, close to the coast. One of the Spanish ships blew up, and another ran aground. The others reached Cadiz heavily

Jaeger Corps Journal

damaged. During the engagement, Prince William Henry [later William IV] was on board Admiral Rodney's ship.

Apr. 16 - A detachment of 250 men, and one non-commissioned officer and fifteen jaegers, under Major [Johann Christian] Dubuy made an excursion into Jersey, toward Hopperstown, where the enemy had assembled, attacked them, and captured six officers and 51 men, and killed another twenty men, without suffering any losses. On the return march, our force was harassed all the way to the boats by the militia, and men who had run from the action. This resulted in two killed and seventeen wounded. Among the wounded was the jaeger non-commissioned officer.

May 1 - During the past night a rebel party of one hundred men attacked a loyalist post at Morrisiana, and took some prisoners.

May 25 - The *Cateret* packet boat arrived today, 39 days out of Falmouth. At Sandy Hook it was attacked by an enemy privateer and had to run onto the sand. The dispatches were brought to Long Island in a boat and thus saved.

May 28 - Colonel [John] Howard of the Guards crossed the North River this evening with 350 men, in order to attack an enemy outpost the other side of Hopperstown. He was to have lain in ambush on the 29th and attacked the post the following night, as the march was too long to complete in one day. The

Jaeger Corps Journal

enemy discovered his presence however, and left the area.

May 29 - The *Iris* came from Charleston with news that that place, as well as the army stationed there, had surrendered on May 12.

Here follows an extract of the journal kept by Captain [Johann] Hinrichs during the siege.

Mar. 20 - The troops are still on James Island, having thrown up several batteries and wait for the man of war, which has their cannon on board, before crossing over the bar. The enemy works with unceasing effort on the city's defenses, a strong point, one battery beside another, springs from the earth like mushrooms. From the point of the city, along the Ashley River, there are 22 shooting sites. The inhabitants on this side of the city to leave their homes and move to the east side, because they have learned from the firing on the enemy ships in the mouth of the Ashley River by our batteries at Fenning's Point, a few days ago, that it would be very easy for us to throw hot shells into the city.

Their forces were reinforced by six hundred men from North Carolina while we were landing. They have regular regiments totaling three thousand men, the remainder were militia, Negroes, and citizens of the city, as well as about one hundred French. Colonel Bland has arrived here in the past few days with the Virginia Light Horse (180) horses, and he and Major

Jaeger Corps Journal

Vernier scouted us between the Ashley River and Randots. All of their infantry were in the city. On the twentieth, only one non-commissioned officer and 25 men, with twelve horses, were the advance post by Ashley River, on the other side of the river. General Prevost had thrown up this "tete de pond" the previous Year to cover his crossing of the river, and immediately began to fire their cannon once again. Also, attack parties from General Patterson's Corps are already allowing themselves to be seen at Stono Ferry. Major Vernier therefore, moved away from our outposts and attacked these parties.

Mar. 21 - As soon as the enemy saw our ships approaching, he pulled all of his back, and assembled them in the Cooper River, between Cooper's Island and the city - schooners, the *Queen of France* frigate, and an old two-decker, all together, Between the sandbank at Fort Johnstone and Sullivan's Island no obstructions could be constructed because the current in the channel, by every ebb and floodtide, is so strong that nothing can withstand its force.

Mar. 22 - As our ships were now over the bar, our batteries on Fenning's Point were finished, our baggage ships and magazines, and our artillery lay by the fortified headquarters, we received orders toward noon to be prepared to march, in order to go up the Ashley River and to cross over it. We were safe from every possible vessel, because the enemy had sent them all into the Cooper River, and opposing these, our batteries on Fenning's Point were strong enough to prevent every undertaking of this sort. We advanced to Church Creek without meeting any enemy resistance. On the other side, by St. Andrew's Church, there was an enemy cavalry detachment. Three companies of Light Infantry had to ford the stream at once. The enemy allowed them to land, fired their carbines, and retreated. The Light Infantry took post in the church, and Captain Ewald was sent with a force of jaegers to support them, and remained there overnight.

The engineers began immediately to reconstruct the bridges which had been burned by the enemy.

Mar. 25 - Major General Patterson with 1,500 men joined us over the Ebenezer, Bamplam, and Wallis Bridges. He had left the Indians [?] at Savannah and brought three troops of the 17th Dragoons, the Legion, and 1st Battalion of the 71st Regiment, the South and North Carolina militia, Ferguson's Corps, and three battalions of Light Infantry. His expectation of recruiting local inhabitants was disappointed, because four hundred rifles meant for them, had been on the Russian merchant transport, which was lost during our sea voyage.

Mar. 29 - Tonight the boats under Captain Tomkins arrived at Major General Leslie's quarters,

Jaeger Corps Journal

and at daybreak embarked the Jaegers, Light Infantry, and the 1st Battalion of English Grenadiers, and landed them at Tom Fuller's. The second division, namely all the grenadiers with two 6-pounders and the Hessian field pieces, crossed over by Tom Trayton's, being followed by the 7th, 33rd, and 71st Regiments of the third division. As soon as everyone had crossed, the baggage was sent back to Ashley Ferry under protection of the 23rd Regiment, the Legion, and the Cavalry, and we set out marching to Ashley Ferry [sic]. The Jaegers had the advance guard, and some enemy cavalry stayed before them. Two miles the other side of Ashley Ferry, we went into camp-headquarters at Quarter's house. The Jaegers were in the front, on the road to Charleston. The Light Infantry was behind them in a half-moon, behind these the English Grenadiers and the Linsingen Battalion. On the front, toward Charleston, were three battalions of Hessian Grenadiers. The 7th Regiment was on the front, toward Cooper's River, with the left wing folded back, to the left of the Hessians. The 23rd and 71st Regiments were in the rear. On the front, toward Dorchester, the pioneers were at the ferry. The enemy was nowhere to be seen. The Jaegers were taken from the brigade of Colonel Webster today, and placed under the direct control of the commanding general.

Mar. 30 - Toward nine o'clock this morning, we broke camp and marched in the same order as

Jaeger Corps Journal

yesterday, to the governor's house before we met the enemy, except for a few light horse. We stopped here because the general, from this house, wanted to reconnoiter the Cooper River, and the defenses of the city on its right wing. Small parties of the enemy were to be seen now, and one of our flankers shot an officer off his horse. At twelve o'clock we again moved forward, but had hardly gone one hundred yards, when some musket shots came from the left side of the road, badly wounding Lord Corney in the body, as he rode in the general's suite, between our advance guard and the corps. We immediately deployed to the left and right of the road. The enemy appeared to be about three hundred men strong. We immediately attached him at a run [in geschwindenJaegerschritten] and drove him back more than a mile and a half to his gatework, a sand pit in the road, which was flanked on the right and left by a swamp. The footpath between the road and Ashley had been obstructed by the enemy with branches. We were already in the swamp which surrounds their flank on the right, and in the front, up to the road, and some would have remained stuck there had we gone on through, and driven them from this open defense work, from which we were less than forty strides away. However, the commanding general himself came and ordered us to remain behind the swamp. We stopped. The Light Infantry marched up behind us. Two companies with a 6-pounder

Jaeger Corps Journal

moved past us on the road, and one company moved to the left of us. The enemy had some good marksmen with whom we exchanged shots. In less than half an hour, a battalion came from the city to reinforce them, and they planted their flag on the defenses. We continued exchanging fire with them for about two hours, when suddenly they deployed and pulled back behind another marsh about one thousand yards further back. Our picket immediately occupied the position, and the general reconnoitered the city. It was about an English mile from here, and all on one plain, no hills thereon, and every house razed, and every tree and bush cut down. Toward evening the enemy general reconnoitered under the protection of two 4-pounders and two battalions of Light Infantry, and advanced as far toward as the gate work. Our pickets moved back about one hundred strides as they advanced with bayonets and cartridge cases. Our weapons were not silenced, and after a period of about one half hour the enemy was no more to be seen. They lost in this action two officers and seven men killed, and three officers and thirty men wounded. Among the first was an adjutant, and among the last, the adjutant general, who had been shot through both cheeks. We had one dead and two wounded. In the evening, we moved into camp on the right wing of the Light Infantry at Gibb's plantation. Behind us stood the British and Hessian Grenadiers from William's

Jaeger Corps Journal

House on the Ashley to the Cooper River. The rear was covered by Colonel Webster, with the 33rd and 71st Regiments. The 23rd marched to Fenning's Point. The Legion and the Cavalry, after a few days, came over here and camped in front of Webster's Brigade. The New York Volunteers were posted at General Leslie's previous quarters on Fenning's Point. Huyne Regiment and the 63rd and 64th Regiments were in a fortified camp on James Island, near the ships and magazines. The South and North Carolina militiamen were behind Tom Rosen's, on the Wappoe Creek.

Mar. 31 - The row galleys which had lain at Ashley Ferry moved down here today on the Wappoe Cheek and the two cannon-carrying boats were placed behind Gibb's plantation to cover communication over the Ashley. Our communication with the ships was a landing behind Gibb's, in line with our camp toward the New York Volunteers on the other side of the river, and from there, over Fenning's Point toward Wappoe Creek, on both sides of which were the North and South Carolina Militia, then along the other side of the Wappoe, through the cut to Huyne's Brigade at Stono, near the magazine. Commencing today, hordes of fortifying material and provisions started coming over, as well as mantlets, partially assembled, fourteen feet long and ten feet high, which had been made in New York. They were put together at Gibb's, where the engineers were gathered.

Jaeger Corps Journal

This is the best, easiest, and surest method of completing batteries, redoubts, etc., in sandy soil. The general and the engineers were on a reconnaissance day and night. The negligence of the enemy in not having filled in the natural ditches, gave them complete protection. During the night, a way was cut through the entanglement, which the enemy had made from sharpened tree limbs, three thousand feet in front of our camp, where Major Montcrief wanted to open his trenches. The mantlets were assembled and today two metal 24-pouncers four iron 24-pounders, two 18l-pounders, a 7-inch and a 9-inch mortar, twelve royal mortars, and two 4 ½ inch barrel mortars were brought over. And, during the night, our first parallel was opened with the completion of three redoubts; the first on the road, and the other two to the left of the road. Each redoubt required sixteen mantlets, which were carried by four hundred workers, who were followed by one hundred men with tools. This totaled 115 laborers on every side, with whom were a staff officer and five captains, a total of five hundred men per redoubt, or 1,500 workers during the night. At twilight, the Light Infantry, under Lieutenant Colonel Abercromby and [Thomas] Dundas moved forward one hundred yards ahead of the workers, in a natural trench. The workers moved out at six o'clock, and a five hundred man reserve, under Colonel Webster, moved into the camp vacated by the 2nd Battalion of

Jaeger Corps Journal

Light Infantry. The engineer captains were assigned to each brigade, and had their assistants with them. The workers marched along the road which led to Gibb's, and left their weapons and knapsacks in front of the camp vacated by the 1st Battalion of Light Infantry, and were assigned to mantlets. At seven-thirty in the evening, Captain Sutherland of the engineers marched out with the 1st Brigade. Shortly thereafter, the other two followed in the utmost silence. The path was marked with stakes on which paper had been fastened. The mantlets were set up, and twelve feet of dirt was shoveled into them. The workers returned, and the Light Infantry occupied them the next day. It was daybreak before the enemy gave the least consideration to placing some hindrance in the way. Toward evening he opened fire with an 18-pounder, from the center of his defenses.

Jaeger Corps Journal

Apr. 2 - The relief force went out every night at twilight, and as soon as they were in place, the workers went out. The three redoubts later were numbered 3, 4, and 5. They were connected this night with connecting trenches and a beginning was made on No. 2 to the right of the road. From the enemy we received a heavy fire. To the left of the road, in line with No. 5, many men made a path leading backward over two marshes.

Apr. 3 - Toward noon, the enemy opened fire with a masked battery of two metal 18-pounders from the demi-bastion to the right of the gate, and during the evening, with two 18-pounders from the front redoubt on his left wing, which raked the road, and No. 3. During this night, the connecting trench to the left of No. 5 was lengthened in a line leading toward the enemy, and on the left wing, a beginning was made on battery No. 6 for nine cannon, with loophole embrasures. No. 2 was improved and on he right, toward the Ashley, a new No. 1 was begun. This one lay closer to the enemy than the others, separated from the first parallel and No. 3 by a swamp, and had a thick swamp, which extended to the Ashley, in front of it.

Apr. 4 - At daybreak, the Jaeger detachment with infantry detachments had to move out, in order to occupy No. 1 and No. 6. Captain Ewald and fifty jaegers were under the command of Lieutenant

Jaeger Corps Journal

Colonel Webster in No. 6. Major von Wurmb and the rest of the jaegers were in No. 1. Captain Hinrichs with fifty jaegers was on picket duty. The enemy maintained a continuous cannonade during the day with 12, 18, and 24-pounders, and five 6-inch howitzers. Two enemy frigates raised anchor toward noon. One came toward No. 6, into which it fired a broadside, but without doing any harm, because the ships lay too deep [lower than the redoubt]. As soon as the ships sailed, Major Moncrief brought a metal 24-pounder to the water with the aid of eighty sailors, close to the left flank of the 2nd Battalion of Light Infantry, and Lieutenant Molo of the Artillery, at the same time, fired two shots into the ship, so that it turned around. Captain Evans of the *Raisonable* arrived with one hundred sailors to occupy a battery, and went into camp in Gibson's garden. This night, No. 6 was enclosed in the rear to prevent being flanked by ships, and platforms were set up. No.1 was improved.

Apr. 5 - The enemy fired without let-up, over seven hundred shots. The general allowed the batteries at Fenning's Point to reply, but in such a manner as not to set the city on fire. These guns fired heavily, being 32-pounders, and caused a terrible confusion in the city. This night, No. 1 was strengthened, two 32-pounders were brought to No. 6, and the platforms in this battery were finished.

Jaeger Corps Journal

Apr. 6 - Today the enemy fired only six cannon balls and six bombs. Seven iron cannon were brought up to the gateway in order, therefore, to be nearer the transports at night. Today, one hundred sailors brought a cannon-carrying boat, pulling it on a ramp with two wheels, from the Ashley River to the Cooper River for use there. At noon, Captain Collins arrived with eighty artillerymen. He had been driven to Bermuda. During the night, the enemy sought to hinder our workers again with a heavy bombardment. No. 6 was furnished with cannon, the embrasures were cut out, and two of them were opened.

Apr. 7 - Only about fifty shots. During the afternoon, a reinforcement of seven hundred men under General Woodford, arrived in the city from Hobcaw's Ferry over the Cooper River. At retreat the enemy fired a feu de joie from all of his batteries, the garrison gave three hurrahs, and all the bells were rung. We believed that the enemy was planning an attack, and ran to our weapons. During the night another path was opened to No. 2, and to the right of No. 2, another battery was begun for twelve heavy cannon. This was called the sailors' battery because the sailors were to occupy it.

Apr. 8 - It was this afternoon that our men of war passed Fort Moultrie. At four o'clock in the afternoon, they came from Five Fathom Hole with the most favorable wind, the strongest flood tide, and covering skies. The admiral led in a jolly-boat, and piloted each ship through. The advance was led by Sir Snape Hammond in the *Roebuck*. At three-thirty he was at the fort, which fired with forty cannon. Nevertheless, the ship proudly came past the fort without turning, despite all the cannonballs, gave it a broadside, and sailed past the fort toward the city, without loss, without stopping, and dropped anchor at Fort Johnstone. Next followed the *Richmond*, which lost its foremast, the *Renown* brought up the rear and as she arrived at the fort, halted, laid the sails back, and fired such a continuous, uninterrupted bombardment, that the entire ship appeared to be on fire. And, in this manner, protected the rear of the squadron. A transport ship ran aground, and was set afire. By six-thirty our ships lay on this side, at anchor, with a loss of seven dead and one midshipman and three sailors wounded. Of these, most were aboard the *Renown*. The frightened enemy fired not a shot while all this transpired, although all our men sprung onto the breastworks of the defenses in order to watch. This night, the sailors' battery was completed. Today the Jaegers were divided into three divisions in front of the army.

Apr. 9 - The enemy fired very little today. An enemy detachment was moved across the Hobcaw. It appeared as if it had two light cannon with it. The enemy ships sought to harass our ships. Therefore, we

Jaeger Corps Journal

directed heavy cannon fire against them. During this afternoon, the commanders of the three Jaeger divisions had to locate advantageous positions in the trenches, where small detachments of Jaegers could be employed with rifles against the enemy. However, the distances were still too great. This night a redoubt, No. 7, was begun about 150 yards ahead of No. 5.

Apr. 10 - Only limited firing, as both sides were working day and night. The enemy opened five new loopholes in his central works against No. 7. This night a powder magazine was laid out in No. 7, and three additional 24-pounders moved in. With these preparations our first parallel was completed, and our cannon commenced firing. The city was called upon to surrender, but this was refused in a polite manner. A blind battery was laid out beside No.7, and to the left of this, a communications trench which, with a re-entering angle, ran on an oblique line to the salient angle at the front of the enemy redoubt on the Cooper River.

Apr. 12 - Captain Hinrichs and twenty jaegers occupied the communications trench, but the distance was still too great for the use of rifles.

In the afternoon, the 23rd and 33rd Regiments and the Legion moved back, in order to cross the Cooper River, and seize the post at Cain Hoy. Our fleet had arrived from New York, and the general did not want to lose a minute in cutting the city off from every

Jaeger Corps Journal

communication.

Apr. 13 - After daybreak, our batteries opened fire to rather good effect. Those on Fenning's Point supported with a restraining fire. No. 2 silenced a battery opposite on the Ashley River. No. 6 fired heated cannon-balls and the city was set afire in three places. The general ordered the firing to be reduced and allowed the enemy to recover. No. 7 suffered the most. During the night, only a few shots were exchanged.

The second parallel was opened tonight. The sap ran in front of No.7, two hundred yards across the swamp, and the parallel was opened for about one hundred yards to the right and left, and had another swamp across the left front. The second parallel lay in the middle, 1,300 feet from the first, and 500 feet from the enemy abatis, and 880 feet from his central defense.

Apr. 14 - Captain Ewald with a mixed force of fifty jaegers and infantry occupied this position. Today there was considerable firing. During the night, the second parallel was extended over two hundred yards to the left, and the path across the swamp was broadened twenty yards in the sap by a mass of workers. We received heavy small arms fire.

Apr. 15 - Captain Hinrichs, fifty jaegers, fifty grenadiers, and fifty light infantry occupied the second parallel. The enemy had constructed counter approaches, occupied with riflemen, with whom we exchanged fire. This night the completed section of the second parallel was strengthened. On the right, the communications trench was extended (in the middle) as far as the road, and in the communications trench to No. 7, a bomb battery for royals and a 7-inch howitzer was constructed and occupied.

Apr. 16 - The Jaeger detachment now occupies, as a general rule, the second parallel. Tonight the sap on the right wing, between Nos. 2 and 3 was opened, and 450 [yards] in front of these, the sap was extended one hundred yards. A natural ditch greatly facilitated this work.

Apr. 17 - Our bombs were to good effect today. This night the communications trench from the right to the left wing was completed, and so the second parallel is finished. Additionally, a sap was begun on the left wing in line with No. 7, as an opening of the third parallel.

Apr. 18 - Captain Hinrichs and Lieutenant [Johann Ernst] von Wintzingerode occupied the third parallel, to the right and left, with sixty jaegers. During the night, the parts of the second parallel, completed last night, were strengthened by improving the defensive positions, as the moonlight was too bright to permit working on the saps in front. A bomb battery was laid out in the second parallel. During the night both sides fired many rounds.

Jaeger Corps Journal

Apr. 19 - Captain [Franz Christian von] Bodungen and Lieutenant [Johannes?] Scheffer occupied the second parallel with sixty jaegers. During the evening, at nine o'clock, our row galleys went from Wappoe to Fort Johnstone, as the admiral needed them for another purpose. The enemy batteries on the Ashley fired heavily. This night the saps to the left of the opening of the third parallel were advanced 136 yards toward the front, and at the same time, a third sap on the right wing was opened to a third parallel.

Apr. 20 - Captain Ewald with thirty jaegers was on the left, and [Ansbach Jaeger] Lieutenant [Jacob Ernst] Kling with thirty on the right. Our riflemen on the left were at a point-blank range from the embrasures of the enemy's advanced redoubt on the Cooper, so that the enemy cannon on our right wing could not easily enfilade from the side. This night the left and right wings of the third parallel were opened, the bomb battery in the second parallel was occupied, and a powder magazine for one 10-inch howitzer was completed. And as we learned from a deserter, that the enemy was planning an attack, a battery in barbette for two 6-pounders and two Hessian field guns was thrown up hastily on the main road, in line with the entrance 160 yards behind the second parallel, and occupied. No attack followed.

Apr. 21 - Captain Hinrichs and Lieutenant von Wintzengerode with sixty jaegers and eighty grenadiers, intermingled, were ordered into the third parallel. The enemy sought to enfilade our flanks from his right and left advanced redoubts. Three flanking field pieces silenced the rifles, as they allowed no one in the embrasures to be able to see. Toward noon, a flag of truce came out in order to surrender. An armistice of six hours was allowed. The enemy's pretensions however, were superfluous, and therefore at ten o'clock in the evening, the discussions were broken off. Our cannon and bomb batteries then fired more heavily than ever before. This night our third parallel was extended. It ran toward the center and forward, so that both wings of the enemy were approached, and at the very end of the left wing of the third parallel, a bomb battery for twelve royals and one 7-inch howitzer was placed and occupied. The same thing was done on the right wing.

 Apr. 22 - Our Jaegers were now well within point-blank range, so that the enemy could not open his embrasures without suffering casualties. This night better saps were extended forward from the right wing, the third parallel was strengthened, a number of traverses were laid out, and a powder magazine for the second advance bomb battery completed.

 Apr. 23 - The enemy riflemen had made a contra-approach on the right wing, and Captain Ewald exchanged shots with them. This night the third parallel of our left wing was extended to the right, to

Jaeger Corps Journal

within ten yards of the enemy gatework and trenches, and on the right wing, extended as far as the enemy glacis.

Apr. 24 - Captain Hinrichs and Lieutenant von Wintzingerode occupied an advance position. The enemy made an attack at daybreak and pushed forward as far as the second parallel at several points, but was beaten back and covered his retreat with an exceptionally heavy fire, with cartridges and pieces of iron, etc. The Jaegers also received many shots fired from behind them from the second parallel. Over one foot of their breastwork was destroyed without their suffering any loss, what good fortune! Except for one Englander, who was slightly wounded by a bayonet. On the right wing, however, where Lieutenant von Wintzingerode was, one man of the Light Infantry was shot dead, five were wounded, and two jaegers were wounded by bayonets, and three were captured. Captain Hinrichs today made two swivels, with which he can fire one hundred musket balls at a time, and in this manner, disturbed the enemy not a little. The signal for an attack was three shots from small arms, bombs, or cannon fire. One of our outposts saw a small party of the enemy, gave the signal, and fired. The workers ran back. The second parallel mistook them for the enemy, and fired, causing everyone to become alarmed. As the smoke prevented further recognition, the firing continued without interruption until two o'clock in the morning before the mistake could be cleared up. From this we had one officer killed, and over fifty wounded, and our workers could accomplish little, or even nothing.

Apr. 25 - There was very little firing. Today Lord Cornwallis with the Irish Volunteers and the North and South Carolina Provincials crossed the Cooper River, in order to join with Colonel Webster. Three boats with cannon were also taken overland to the Cooper, where they captured several enemy schooners. Major General Patterson took Lord Cornwallis' place, coming from James Island to serve in the line. During the previous night, work already commenced was continued. Several traverses were constructed and seventy passages leading forward against the enemy's half-moon battery, in contra approaches, were dug.

Apr. 26 - Firing was at intervals. Our battery No. 7 suffered the most, being poorly constructed, and all the embrasures were destroyed. The admiral did everything possible to find a way so that he could bring the ships up the Cooper River. However, it was simply not possible without losing the ships. In the center of the third parallel, a bomb battery for seven royals and one 10-inch bomb mortar was established. On the left, a battery for two 12-pounders to be used against the front redoubt was built, and another for four 24-pounders was set up to be used against the demi-bastion and the hornwork.

Jaeger Corps Journal

Apr. 27 - Our workers now work half by night and half by day. The Jaegers and the Light Infantry lie behind sandbags, and there are always some with cocked weapons, in the event anyone should appear in an embrasure. The enemy tries to camouflage themselves as herdsmen, but when this happens they are immediately fired upon. During the afternoon Lord Cornwallis came to Hobcaw Ferry. The enemy abandoned it, leaving four cannon behind. Three row galleys with 18-pounders took position in Spencer's Inlet and exchanged fire with the enemy bridge battery on Mount Pleasant. This night the batteries in the third parallel were finished and occupied. No. 7 was completely abandoned and destroyed.

Apr. 28 - Commencing today efforts were made to divert the water from the enemy ditches. The defenses were improved and traverses were constructed leading to the third paralleled, to prevent enfilading. Since we were so close to his abatis, the enemy burned numerous filled casks between the first and second abatis throughout the night, which was meant to hinder our approach.

Apr. 29 - Moderate firing. The dam was destroyed by gunfire. The water ran off three-fourths of an inch an hour, and the next day, one inch, so that the ten foot wide ditches might soon be dry. Our workers did very little.

Apr. 30 - Throughout this day the enemy fired

Jaeger Corps Journal

quite a bit. The admiral landed with two hundred marines on Lampier's Point, where he found seven cannon, and established a battery. Major Ferguson made a reconnaissance from Hobcaw and believed he had found the enemy. Therefore, he engaged the marines for a quarter of an hour. The *Comet* galley and the *Renown* wished to approach the bridge battery. The *Comet* grounded fast, the *Renown* also, but was able to get loose. The galley however, was a complete loss. This night we worked on the traverses. The right wing battery was occupied by the marines with two 24-pounders.

Jaeger Corps Journal

May 1 - Nos. 2 and 6 were completely unoccupied. Therefore the enemy gave considerable effort to destroy our front defenses, and threw many bombs. This caused us the loss of some jaegers. During the night, the battery at the enemy's lattice work was improved, and provided with eighteen foot thick traverses. Also the powder magazines, in the center near the bomb battery, were completed.

May 2 - The 64th Regiment crossed back over the Cooper River, with 23 prisoners, among which was the governor's son. The parallel on the left was strengthened, and the battery for two 12-pounders was provided with traverses. The sappers worked with good success on the diversion from the canal.

May 3 - Some deserters came in, but their stories were not in agreement. The French engineer recently sent here by General Washington has commenced closing the rear of their defenses. The horn work in the middle was nearly finished. On April 30 the enemy lost their best bombardier, a major of artillery, killed by a rifle ball. This night another powder magazine was completed, and the trenches behind the battering ram of the front parallel were made.

May 4 - This morning the Jaeger detachment, as usual, marched out, but a cannon-ball landed this side of No. 3 and felled seven of them. One lost a leg, another was hit in the thick part of his leg by the cannon-ball, and five others were wounded by branches broken off by the shot. During the afternoon, still another jaeger was shot. At night, on the extreme left wing of the second parallel, close to a swamp, by the Cooper River, a battery for two cannon was laid out.

May 5 - Captain Ewald went by another route close to the Ashley River today to enter the trenches, because deserters had informed the enemy of the time and route of the relief force, and at this time had the way well defended. This night the battery in the second parallel was completed, and others improved.

May 6 - The enemy could not fire very much because our rifle fire kept him behind his defenses. However, at night he fired all the more heavily, and destroyed much of the too lightly constructed forward defenses. During this night our batteries were all completed and provided with ammunition. At one o'clock an alarm was sounded in the city.

May 7 - Today was spent moving up ammunition, and the sailors' battery at the gate defense was improved. Toward noon we received the news that Fort Moultrie had been captured. Ferguson had landed on one side, and the marines from the frigate *Richmond* on the other, in order to capture the bridge battery, which was closed in the rear for purposes of strength, and which was defended by the enemy captain, Williams, with about twenty men. As soon as he learned of the marine landing, he thought it was some sailors who wanted to obtain cattle, and followed them with his troops, in order to chase them away. Major Ferguson had also landed, and captured Williams and all of his troops without firing a shot, and entered the battery, which was open, with Fort Moultrie being unaware of the danger. As soon as Ferguson had occupied the battery, at two o'clock in the morning, he called upon the fort to surrender. The commandant of the fort was very disturbed by the completely unexpected loss of the bridge battery, and surrendered. In the fort there was a remarkable supply of provisions: cattle, bread, meal, etc. The importance of occupying this fort was obvious for our ships, and our direct communications with them by way of Fort Johnstone.

This afternoon we received a report of a second attack on the enemy cavalry by ours on the Santee, near Hell's Hole Swamp. The first time, Tarleton had attacked them on the Cooper, and now the rest of them had been eliminated.

May 8 - Our battering rams were all completed and the embrasures opened, and once again the city was called upon to surrender. The discussions lasted until six o'clock in the evening. Several points were firmly established, but then suddenly broken off. At eight o'clock in the evening, the armistice ended, and the enemy rang all the bells, and after shouting hurrah three times, made such an uninterrupted firing as never before. This night our workers approached the right parallel from the left wing, directly through the enemy trenches, and twenty yards behind the abatis.

May 9 - This morning our batteries and bombs commenced a continuous fire. The enemy front redoubt on the left wing demolished one of our 24-pounders, which was firing upon them, with the first salvo, but even so, another replaced it so quickly, that in two hours, the battery was silenced and completely destroyed. The firing lasted all day.

May 10 - A lot of bombs were thrown. In the last fourteen days, the enemy has fired less. The 10-inch howitzer was brought up, which had been captured at Fort Moultrie, and placed in the right side of the third parallel.

May 11 - The enemy withstood the fire until midday and answered it. Toward midday, he sent a flag of truce, which because of the heavy firing, could not be seen, and therefore had to return. At two o'clock in the afternoon, he raised a large white flag at the horn defenses and sent a second flag, by which he surrendered the city on the conditions we had offered.

An armistice was extended to him. At eleven o'clock, the capitulation was agreed upon.

May 12 - Although the surrender of the city was firmly agreed upon, still the Jaeger detachment had to move out as usual. At twelve o'clock there was still

Jaeger Corps Journal

no possibility of bringing the militia together and under guard. As soon as everything was finally agreed upon and the articles were signed, the gate defenses were torn down by the engineers, and the bridge relaid. Thereupon, Captain Hinrichs, with one noncommissioned officer crossed over and established a post on the other side, since the enemy guards had pulled back. At two o'clock, General Leslie rode at the head of two grenadier companies, namely one from the 7th Regiment, under Lieutenant Colonel Hope, and the other from the Linsingen Battalion, under Lieutenant Colonel Linsingen. Each company with its field guns entered the city. Behind these followed the royal colors. At the gate, Major General Lincoln, mounted, and Major General Moultrie, on foot, waited and surrendered the city. As the English Grenadiers passed through the gate, the hauteboists played "God Bless King George". The Grenadiers then took possession of the horn defenses, and planted their cannon at the place d'arms, opposite the city. Then twenty jaegers and twenty light infantrymen pulled a chain between the abatis and the outer defenses, so that the enemy garrison, all of whom were to surrender their arms, could place them there. The whole occupation force had to remain under arms, and all the jaegers and light infantry moved forward into the second parallel, until the enemy had laid down their arms. As soon as the Jaegers took post, the enemy force came out. They had permission to march out with music playing, and covered flags. Also they could play no English march, but only a Turkish one. First came the artillery corps, 1st and 2nd South Carolina, 1st and 2nd North Carolina, and 1st and 2nd Virginia Continentals, then the French and Spanish Free Corps. As soon as the weapons were stacked, the royal flag was raised at the gate, and saluted with 22 cannon shots from our camp. The 7th, 63rd, 64th, and 43rd Regiments marched into the city during the afternoon, and the two latter camped on the market place. The others occupied the defenses. The prisoners were then put in barracks under guard. The officers, who had been allowed to retain their side arms, had permission to go about the city. A large amount of artillery was captured: 290 iron and 21 metal cannon, and some large and small howitzers and mortars, as well as those still on board the frigates *Providence* and *Ranger*, as well as other enemy ships lying in the harbor.

May 15 - A powder magazine exploded due to the negligence of the English artillerymen, resulting in many men, wagons, and horses, etc., being lost.

During the afternoon, the Ditfurth and Huyne Regiments moved into the city.

Therefore, for more than one reason, this important post was in our hands, and the army made prisoners of war. It was the warehousing place for

Jaeger Corps Journal

French-American trade. It was the only secure harbor of the two fertile provinces, and was captured by England with a small force, against the strongest defenses, in as much as a sandbar, which by the highest floodtide had only a depth of seventeen to nineteen and three-fourths feet, enclosed the entire harbor entrance, and where every ship with more than forty guns, found it impossible to cross over the bar without the strenuous unloading of the lower rows. [End of Hinrich's account]

***

June 5 - The army, under Lieutenant General von Knyphausen was ordered to march tomorrow, leaving behind all equipment, wives, sick persons, etc. A detachment of one hundred jaegers, under Captain von Wangenheim, was to remain at Morris Hill, also.

June 6 - At two o'clock in the morning, the Jaeger Corps and the Guards were embarked in eight sloops at Turtle Bay on the East River, and set sail at one o'clock, passing New York, where the rest of the army was also embarking, and dropped anchor near Cole's Ferry on Staten Island. Here, at four o'clock the troops in 56 sloops and schooners had come together, lifted anchor, and sailed to Decker's Ferry. However, because the wind and the tide were contrary, they reached the ferry only at seven o'clock in the evening. (Otherwise a very short distance.) The division of

Jaeger Corps Journal

Major General Stirling (37th, 38th, Leib and Landgraf Regiments) was in flatboats, and had orders to land at Elizabethtown Point to attack the enemy troops there (the Jersey Brigade of Major General Maxwell). The army was to follow by water if the wind had not made it necessary to land on Staten Island, and to march to Elizabethtown Point, where on the morning of

June 7 - at daybreak, they were transported across in forty flatboats in the following order:

I. Major General Mathews Division--seventeen companies, two 6-pounders, the 22nd and 57th Regiments, 1st and 4th Battalions of Skinner's [Pro-[vincials].

II. Major General Tryon's Division--Buenau Regiment, the Jaegers, Guards, and the Engineers.

III. Major General Hachenberg's Division--43rd Regiment, Ansbach Regiment, Bose Regiment, and two 3-pounders.

IV. Major General Lossberg's Division--Donop Regiment, 17th Dragoons, Mounted Jaegers, and Artillery.

The crossing was not finished until three o'clock in the afternoon.

In the meantime, Major General Stirling's Brigade landed at two o'clock in the night, in order to drive the enemy out of Elizabethtown. Just at the start, General Stirling was wounded, and gave the command over to Colonel von Wurmb, who followed the enemy to the other side of the town. As soon as General Mathews' Division landed, it marched off and joined with Colonel von Wurmb on the other side of Elizabethtown. The enemy defended himself during his retreat toward Springfield and challenged every defile energetically. The Jaeger Corps at that time, because of the lost people to the various detachments and the Cavalry, consisted of only three hundred men. As soon as its turn came, following the transfer across of the Buenau Regiment, it followed Major General Mathews with a forced march, and joined with him just after he had driven the enemy from the steep defile at Connecticut Farms. Here the army was assembled and General Mathews therefore established a post. The Jaegers were to take position in the front, on the Springfield Road, and had the task of driving the enemy from the terrain which he still held in that area. This occurred with the loss of some wounded, and the Corps took post in a corner of a woods which had thick growth on the right and left, which had to be occupied by the detachments, and to their front at about six hundred yards, there were houses. The enemy took position behind these and had to be dislodged, which nevertheless, occurred with the loss of some wounded, and the Corps established another post there, which was as disadvantageously located as the first one. The enemy continued to fire and pressed forward several times with the bayonet and new

Jaeger Corps Journal

reinforcements, but was always repulsed until finally driven from the field in our front, where both sides left men dead. As often as he was beaten back, so often he returned with a fresh attack, and this continued until about one o'clock, when suddenly the grenadier company of the Light Infantry was detached to support the Jaegers, and to drive the enemy back as far as Springfield. This occurred, and the enemy retreated under cover of his regimental cannon, which began to fire. Thereupon General von Knyphausen ordered a halt. Then two English 6-pounders came up and began firing on the enemy, who had marched up on the other side of the river, and replied with fire from two cannon until about four o'clock, when the general ordered us to draw back to our former position. The army meantime had set up camp and the Jaegers occupied the previously described post in the corner of the woods. The pickets were posted to the right and left and to the front, in the houses. This had hardly taken place when they were attacked by the enemy. The Corps moved out to support them, drove the enemy back a great distance, and Lieutenant Colonel von Wurmb ordered that the houses lying in our front be set afire. This, and the arrival of our two cannon at about seven o'clock, and also one regimental gun from the Buenau Regiment, which was attached to us to cover our left flank (because the terrain was too extensive for the Jaegers), kept the enemy's respect thereafter. From the various attacks, we had one officer [Ansbach Jaeger] (Lieutenant [Friedrich] Ebenauer), two non-commissioned officers, and two jaegers dead; three officers, three non-commissioned officers, and 44 jaegers wounded. Our people had been fully engaged, and had exchanged fire the entire day with the enemy, whose losses could not be determined. However, we found several dead officers and many privates, and made five prisoners.

At dusk, deserters reported that Washington had broken camp at Morristown at eleven o'clock this morning, and was still expected at Springfield this evening. This corresponded with the comments of the prisoners, and was reported to headquarters. At eleven o'clock in the evening, the army broke camp and marched back toward Elizabethtown.

A strong thunderstorm made the march difficult. At daybreak, the army re-passed the city and camped on Elizabethtown Point, close to the water.

June 8 - The baggage was taken back to Staten Island, followed by the Jaegers, since they had no more ammunition. The Cavalry was also shipped over to Staten Island. The remaining troops however, camped in such a position as to invite an enemy attack on the Point. Toward ten o'clock the enemy appeared in force, and attacked the 22nd Regiment, which had to soften the initial enemy advantage. As however, the Buenau and Ansbach Regiments moved up to support,

Jaeger Corps Journal

the enemy pulled back with a loss of many men, and was pursued as far as the city. It was not the entire enemy army, but a corps under General Stirling, which had been detached from the army in order to observe us.

June 9 - The Cavalry was transferred to the army, likewise the baggage. Sixty jaegers under Captain Lorey were provided with the Corps' remaining ammunition, and joined the army on the special orders of the generals, in order to occupy the outer posts, and to control the enemy flankers, who had done the army great injury. The rifle fire fully accomplished the desired result, in that upon their arrival and their first fire, the enemy posts were withdrawn.

June 10 - The Jaeger Corps had worked steadily on the ammunition, and this morning at ten o'clock, rejoined the army. Immediately after their arrival, various changes in the dispositions of the army were undertaken. The Jaegers were posted close to the city, and kept pickets therein.

June 11 - The Jaeger Corps moved further into the city and advanced its pickets up to the bridge, which led across the river and to the outer part of the city, on whose further banks the enemy posts were located. The enemy army was at Springfield and Connecticut Farms, with an advance corps near Livingston's house. During the night, our pickets were withdrawn somewhat to about the middle of the city. A floating

Jaeger Corps Journal

bridge for communications was built across the water to connect with Staten Island, and protected by a strong point at the head of the bridge.

June 12 - The pickets and especially the outposts kept up a steady fire. Through the opportunity of a flag of truce which came over, Lieutenant Colonel von Wurmb forbade such [the exchange of fire], it being of little value. The enemy officer, who was the adjutant general for General Stirling, also promised to change this [the exchange of fire]. But nothing changed.

June 13 - Our mounted jaegers, at seven o'clock in the evening, crossed the bridge to Newark to attack the enemy cavalry picket, which however, was warned in time and departed. N.B. It is nearly impossible to surprise the enemy at any time because every house which one passes is, so to speak, an advance post, because the farmer or his son, also his wife and daughter, shoot a rocket up or run along the footpaths to report to the enemy.

June 14 - The enemy picket has pulled back because it has been seriously injured by the rifle fire.

June 15 - A jaeger was shot dead at the outpost. We laid ambushes before our outposts, and were able to deliver heavy fire on the enemy patrols. Both armies remained quiet in their camps, and not the least movement was made.

June 16 - Today we received news that General Clinton with a part of the troops from Charleston had returned. We expected an enemy attack, and our pickets were therefore strengthened. The pickets had orders in case of a serious attack not to leave their posts until they had set fire to the houses, which would have seriously hindered the enemy from attacking us on this side.

June 17 - As opposed to our expectation, everything was quiet.

June 18 - This morning at two o'clock the enemy made an attack on our pickets at both bridges, and fired a light cannon on the left flank from the other side of the river, into our Cavalry and the Donop Regiment, but pulled back as a result of the following resistance, without undertaking further action.

June 19 - At ten o'clock General Clinton arrived at the army, and reconnoitered dispositions as well as the enemy's outposts. The troops which came with him from Charleston (British and Hessian Grenadiers, Light Infantry, and 42 jaegers and rangers) were debarked on Staten Island, and camped there in order to refresh themselves.

June 20&21 - Nothing noteworthy. Both armies quiet, without the least movement.

June 22 - The Queen's Rangers rejoined the army today and camped on the right flank of the Jaeger Corps, and are now under the orders of Lieutenant Colonel von Wurmb. This afternoon, the Cavalry went across the wooden bridge in order to surprise the enemy's pickets. These pulled back into the woods and only five men fell into the hands of the foot jaegers. A Queen's Ranger was killed, and two jaegers wounded.

June 23 - At three o'clock in the morning, the following regiments and corps marched toward Springfield 1) Major General Mathews' Division--Rangers, Guards, Landgraf Regiment, 1st and 4th Battalions of Skinner's Provincials. 2) Major General Tryon's Column--Jaegers, 37th and 38th Regiments, Leib, Bose, and Ansbach Regiments. The Rangers arrived at the enemy's outposts, which at once withdrew toward Connecticut Farms, where Colonel [Elias] Dayton's Regiment for some time, defended the advantageous pass at that place, and then retired toward Springfield. The royal troops formed on the heights this side of Springfield (where the Jaegers had been engaged on the seventh of the month). General Mathews commanded the right wing and was to cross the river in order to seize a height lying on the enemy's left front, while General Tryon was to force the bridge, which led directly to Springfield, and was defended by two columns. The 38th Regiment was given this task. The Jaegers divided themselves to the right and left of the bridge, waded through the water, which was rather deep, and drove the enemy from the opposite shore with a heavy fire. At this moment, also, the regiment pressed onto the bridge and drove off the enemy posted there. He retreated through the city and joined a strong corps on the opposite side of the heights, leaving behind numerous casualties of dead and wounded. The Jaegers had two dead, and two officers and twenty men wounded in this attack. The 38th Regiment had a captain killed and several men wounded. General Mathews crossed the river with very little resistance. The army halted in Springfield. The enemy army marched onto Short's Hill and fired some cannon at us. The Jaeger Corps was posted at the other side of Springfield, and exchanged fire with the enemy for more than an hour, during which Lieutenant Colonel von Prueschenck and Captain von Roeder [possibly Friedrich Wilhelm, an Ansbach officer], as well as several jaegers, were wounded. Thereafter the army marched back, after setting fire to Springfield. The Jaegers composed the rear guard, and could hardly make their way between the fires of the already collapsing houses. The enemy followed us on foot and pressed closely upon our rear, so that we continuously had to face about and return their fire. In this manner, we lost additional men, and two miles from the old camp near Elizabethtown, were relieved by the 37th Regiment. Each regiment again took its former position. The enemy also did the same, and put out pickets. After our arrival in camp, we received orders to send our baggage to Staten Island at once, and at twelve o'clock all the troops

Jaeger Corps Journal

followed. The Jaegers were the rear guard, and crossed the bridge, which was immediately broken up, at twelve-thirty. The Donop Regiment, which was posted at the head of the bridge, was picked up in flat boats after the pontoons used to construct the bridge had all been taken away. The army lay on Staten Island along the main road until it was day.

June 24 - The Jaegers, Guards, and Rangers were embarked today, and sailed up the North River to Philipse's House. Here they met, at anchor, the troops which had come from Charleston, and on June 25--all debarked and entered the familiar camp near Philipse's House.

July 1 - The army remained quietly encamped. Washington, as usual, after we had vacated the Jerseys, moved toward West Point, in order to cover the Highlands. His forward outposts were on the Croton River.

July 16 - We received news that Admiral Graves had arrived at New York with six ships of the line.

He had followed a French fleet, with six thousand men on board, which entered Rhode Island.

July 18 - The Jaeger Corps patrolled as far as Sing Sing without meeting any enemy.

July 19 - The royal war fleet made preparations to engage the French in Rhode Island.

July 20 - Most of the army was ordered to embark at Frog's Neck tomorrow, in order to go to Rhode

Jaeger Corps Journal

Island, as the war fleet had already sailed for that place today, in order to attack the French.

July 21 - Today at ten o'clock General [James] Irvine, with 1,800 men, attacked a blockhouse on the other side of the North River near Bull's Ferry, which was occupied by our loyalists, and which had been built by them for their use when sent to the Jersey side to cut wood, and to provide enemy deserters with a secure crossing point. The blockhouse was commanded by Captain [Thomas] Ward, whose command consisted of 84 men. Irvine bombarded the blockhouse from ten o'clock in the morning until one-thirty without effect, and then sought to take it by storm. He advanced as close as the abatis, but was then driven back three miles, with a loss of ninety men. The loyalists had very little ammunition and in the end, were firing small shot such as used for duck hunting, but which did great damage. More than seventy 6-pound cannon-balls stuck in the blockhouse, or had gone through it, but the loyalists still had only five dead and wounded.

July 23 - Today the troops at Frog's Neck went on board. Only three hundred jaegers, under Captain Ewald went on the expedition (because Lieutenant Colonel von Prueschenck was wounded, and Major von Wurmb was sick). The rest of the army marched to Kingsbridge and camped on the Heights of Hotham under the command of Major General Tryon. These

Jaeger Corps Journal

were composed of the rest of the Jaegers, 57th and 80th Regiments, Guards, 17th Dragoons, Hussars, and loyalists.

July 27 - This morning an enemy party entered Philipse's House and plundered it. A jaeger patrol under Lieutenant von Wintzingerode went out this evening and lay in ambush in the Philipse's church all night, but no enemy appeared.

July 31 - Our fleet returned from Huntington and lay at anchor at Whitestone, because the French had already fortified themselves on Rhode Island, and Admiral Arbuthnot did not consider it advisable to attack them there.

Jaeger Corps Journal

Aug. 1 - This evening the field equipment for the troops which lay at anchor at Whitestone was sent away as they are to go into camp on Long Island.

Aug. 2 - The troops which were camped at Hotham Heights, today marched into the line at Kingsbridge. The Jaegers entered camp on Morris Hill.

Aug. 6, 7, & 8 - We made daily patrols without encountering the enemy. Washington crossed the North River again with his army, into Jersey, and Admiral Arbuthnot lies in Gardner's Bay, on the east end of Long Island, in order to observe the French in Rhode Island.

Aug. 12 - On the Harlem Plain, right on Snake Hill, a new defensive position has been laid out, in order to prevent the enemy crossing the creek from Morrisiana, near Harlem.

Aug. 21 - Lieutenant Colonel von Wurmb, with sixty mounted and one hundred foot jaegers, made a patrol to Dobb's Ferry, in order to reconnoiter the enemy camp at Tappan.

Aug. 25 - An enemy detachment seized the post at the former Fort Lee and the blockhouse at Bull's Ferry, abandoned by the loyalists, and installed several cannon in them. The enemy army is presently camped at Paramus and English Neighborhood.

Sept. 10 - Today we received reports that on

Jaeger Corps Journal

August 16, near Camden, Lord Cornwallis had defeated General Gates. This affair occurred at daybreak. Both armies had broken camp, each to attack the other. They met during the night, while on the march, and after a brief skirmish between the advance troops, both armies halted, and the action began at daybreak. The American army became confused, and was defeated. Gates lost five cannon, nine flags, and all his baggage and ammunition, most of which was taken from him during the pursuit by the Cavalry. Also the Cavalry and Light Infantry sent in pursuit of the enemy by the general, captured four hundred men. Gates' total losses amounted to eight hundred dead and wounded, including Major General [Johann] Kalb and Major General Rutherford, as well as twelve hundred prisoners. General Gates, because of the misfortune and reportedly because of the confusion during the retreat, has been suspended from command, and replaced by General [Nathanael] Green. On the other hand, had General Gates been successful, the inhabitants who had made a sort of oath, would have taken up weapons and burned all the royal magazines. This however, was prevented by his flight, and several leaders of these desperate measures were arrested.

Sept. 16 - Admiral Rodney arrived at Sandy Hook from the West Indies today, with ten ships of the line.

Sept. 27 - The enemy Major General [Benedict]

Jaeger Corps Journal

Arnold arrived in New York today. He had found it necessary to take flight in the *Vulture* sloop of war, which lay at Stony Point, because Major [John] Andre, with whom he had been discussing the handing over of the defenses of West Point, which Arnold then commanded, had been exposed at Terrytown during his return, and papers were found on him, which he had received from Arnold.

Oct. 3 - Despite the strenuous efforts which General Clinton exerted to save Major Andre, his adjutant general, Andre was hanged yesterday at twelve o'clock in the enemy camp at Tappan. General Washington held a court-martial in which all the rebel generals were present, concerning Andre. He had been three days with General Arnold, had seen the defenses himself, had developed and participated in the planning of the manner in which they were to be put into the King's hand, and had been captured in civilian clothing during his return to New York. His life was forfeit. The specific plan was: Arnold already had torn down the palisades in the outer wall in various defensive positions, which were to have been replaced with new, better, and stronger materials. He would then take the troops out of the defenses and march against us, off to one side, where he could easily be cut off from the fort. The English Light Infantry therefore, had already marched from Long Island to the Jaeger camp, in order to be able to march with us the moment that Andre returned.

Oct. 7 - Major General Arnold has been made a brigadier general, and has received a new corps of foot and mounted personnel called the American Legion, to which, by public proclamation, he has invited all American officers and soldiers.

Major General Leslie embarked today with the Guards and some other troops in order to sail to Virginia.

Oct. 10 - A detachment of one hundred jaegers under Captain von Roeder was sent to join Major General Leslie, in order to sail with the expledition, also.

Oct. 17 - The London fleet arrived today with the recruits, which increased the Ansbach Jaeger Corps to four hunderd men, and over which Captain Waldenfels has been given command.

Oct. 28 - The army entered winter quarters as in previous years. The Jaegers were assigned to Westbury, Jericho, and Herricks, and manned the outer posts on the eastern end of Long Island. The enemy army will spend the winter, part at Morristown and part at West Point, the headdquarters at West Point.

Dec. 9 - From Carolina we hear that Major Ferguson, who commanded eight hundred militiamen, was attacked on October 7, near Kings's Mountain by the enemy, General [Ortho A.] Williams with 2,500 men, and in a hard fought battle, Williams, as well as

Jaeger Corps Journal

Ferguson, was killed. Ferguson's troops surrendered after the action ended. The rebels held a field court-martial, and hung some officers and the colonel of the English militia.

Dec. 10 - General Ewald [sic Arnold?] embarked today with the 80th Regiment, Rangers, Robinson's Corps, and about one hundred Jaegers, under Captain Ewald, in order to go to Virginia, because General Leslie had departed from there, and gone to Carolina to join Lord Cornwallis.

Jaeger Corps Journal
1781

Jan. 4 - The army received orders to be prepared to march. The Pennsylvania Brigade, which like the rest of the army had received neither pay nor good provisions until now, revolted on January 1. Everyone, with the exception of the officers, was determined to go home. Major General Wayne, who commanded them, exerted himself strenuously in an effort to get the troops to return to duty, and had made them great promises, but to no avail. They chose officers from among their non-commissioned officers, and a certain Sergeant Williams accepted the overall command. They seized four cannon and all the provisions and marched to Bordertown, having decided as one, not to return to duty until they were given their pay, their discharges, and good provisions.

Jan. 5 - At seven o'clock this morning an express brought orders for the Jaeger Corps to march at daybreak. We moved out at nine o'clock and marched to the far side of Jamaica, where we spent the night in barns. The Hessian Grenadiers had vacated Jamaica and marched to Graves End.

Jan. 6 - The Jaeger Corps marched at seven o'clock through Flatbush over Graves End, to Denyse's Ferry. There they were embarked on schooners and at dusk, landed at Decker's Ferry, on Staten Island. We found the Hessian Grenadiers and the Light Infantry quartered there, and we received

Jaeger Corps Journal

two barns for our entire Corps. General Clinton himself was there in order to see what the outcome of the revolt would be, and if there was not some advantage to be obtained. He had, to this end, also sent emissaries to make all possible offers to Williams.

Jan. 7 - We expected at any moment to cross over into Jersey, but we hoped in vain.

Jan. 8 - The new rebels under Williams have reportedly increased to three thousand men. They are now at Princeton, and with Congress now in Trenton, await a deputation sent to them.

Jan. 9 - The Hessian Grenadiers are returning to Long Island, and will camp at Graves End, a sign that General Clinton is not wiling to enter Jersey. The Jaegers therefore were assigned a few more barns.

Jan. 10 - Unfortunately two of our spies who were to take General Clinton's overtures to Mr. Williams, were discovered because of their carelessness, by the militia, and hanged on the spot.

Jan. 11 - General Clinton went to New York and returned on the twelfth. The thunderstorms are strong and unpleasant, and the troops in the open barns are greatly exposed to the same.

Jan. 15 - Williams with his troops and the deputation from Congress have not come to a complete understanding. Meantime however, it appears the event will have a favorable outcome, because a subscription has been begun in Philadelphia

Jaeger Corps Journal

to raise gold and silver with which to pay the soldiers.

Jan. 16 - General Clinton with his suite returned to New York, and Major General [William] Philipps commands on Staten Island.

Jan. 20 - A part of the Jersey brigade has likewise revolted. The situation however, was quickly resolved and two of the rebel leaders were hanged.

Feb. 2 - General Arnold has landed at Richmond in Virginia, burned all the magazines there, as well as a cannon foundry, and has gone to Portsmouth where he will establish a post.

As our merchant fleet sailed for England today, the French sent out three ships of the line from Rhode Island to observe them, and at the same time to reconnoiter the Chesapeake. Our fleet was convoyed by four warships. However the French fell in with a fleet which was being escorted by the *Romulus* of 44-guns, coming from Charleston, and captured the *Romulus*, as well as several transport ships.

Feb. 10 - Ten ships of the line and ten regiments have arrived in the West Indies to reinforce Admiral Rodney. Admiral [Sir Samuel] Hood has convoyed this fleet from England.

Feb. 16 - The packet boat with the December dispatches arrived in New York today. There is very little news from Europe.

Feb. 17 - From the *Halifax*, with the November packet by way of Charleston, we hear that Lieutenant

Jaeger Corps Journal

Colonel Tarleton has been defeated in an action with General Morgan. Tarleton was detached from Lord Cornwallis to follow General Morgan, who commands the enemy light infantry and a militia corps. Morgan retreated ahead of Tarleton until he took a firm post in the Cowpens. Tarleton, therefore, became excited and considered Morgan trapped. Tarleton camped the night of the seventeenth in the vacated camp of the enemy, and attacked him the next morning with his usual rashness. Morgan had his militia in front and these, as he had expected, fled. Tarleton pursued eagerly, maybe not in the best order, and immediately attacked the well-aligned infantry. They withstood his attack and completely routed the British force. A part of the English cavalry escaped. The infantry however, for the most part, was captured. Likewise, two cannon, two flags, 35 baggage wagons, eight hundred weapons, one field forge, etc., were lost. This unfortunate affair greatly upset Lord Cornwallis, who, nevertheless, marched against General Greene.

General Washington in celebration of this success allowed his army to fire a feu de joie, and made the utmost of the event. By this opportunity he announced the recent revolts in official orders, and threatened the most drastic punishment should such events occur in the future.

Feb. 18 - General Leslie has joined with Lord Cornwallis. Our Jaeger detachment, on January 5, was

Jaeger Corps Journal

at Camden according to reports received from Captain Roeder. Lieutenant Colonel von Wurmb, with sixty mounted and one hundred foot jaegers, went to Schmidttown on the east end of Long Island early today, in order to protect a party of loyalists on a wood-cutting detail. The loyalists were partially fortified against attack by New Englanders, which according to reports, was to be expected. The New Englanders however, having received news of the arrival of the Jaegers, did not attack but remained away from the woodcutters--a result of their having good friends on this island who give them reports, and which therefore make it nearly impossible to surprise them in this manner.

Feb. 19 - The British and Hessian Grenadiers, Light Infantry, 42nd and 76th Regiments received orders to be ready to embark.

Mar. 6 - The Grenadiers were not embarked. However the Light Infantry, 87th and 76th Regiments, and the Hereditary Prince Regiment, under the command of Major General Philipps, were. And as the reports from Carolina indicate that Lord Cornwallis has advanced into North Carolina, and detached four hundred men to occupy Wilmington, it is assumed, not without some basis, that General Philipps will sail to Virginia in order to make a diversion in support of Lord Cornwallis.

Mar. 12 - Yesterday the French fleet sailed from

Rhode Island. It has two thousand men on board, and it is believed that they are meant for the Chesapeake, as the Marquis de Lafayette has been detached from Washington's army with two thousand men, in order to co-operate with them.

The English fleet followed the French on March 13 and therefore General Philipps, with the troops he had on board, could not sail, but remained at Sandy Hook awaiting further orders.

Mar. 16 - Today war was declared against Holland. We learned at the same time that on February 3, Admiral Rodney had taken possession of Eustacia. Rodney arrived before Eustacia on February 3, flying the French flag. The inhabitants, knowing nothing different, believed the fleet would sail against the English islands, but they were surprised when the English flag was displayed, and at the same time were called upon to surrender the island. The governor requested a period of four hours to consider this, which was granted. However, during the time also, two thousand men were landed. And, under this threat, the island surrendered at discretion. One hundred thirty-eight French, Spanish, American, and Holland ships, among which many were richly laden, were captured. And with these, a Holland frigate which saluted Admiral Rodney, and then struck its flag. The dispatches of the admiral, in which he was notified of the war against Holland, were dated

Jaeger Corps Journal

January 8. Thereafter we sent a small squadron in pursuit of the Holland fleet, which had sailed a short time previously, with 25 ships. These were met after several days, and after a brief engagement of a quarter of an hour, surrendered, the Holland admiral having been killed.

The loss for the Hollanders, as well as the other enemies of England, as a result of their warehouses being on this neutral island is devastating, and a rich treasure for the English sea power.

Mar. 20 - Yesterday General Philipps sailed.

Mar. 27 - Admiral Arburhnot yesterday sent an express boat to inform General Clinton that he had fallen in with the French fleet under [Paul Francois Jean, Comte] de Barras off the Virginia Capes on March 16, and engaged it. He gives the following account thereof:

At daybreak on the sixteenth, the frigate *Iris* made the signal for having discovered several ships in the distance to eastward, and was then ordered by a signal from the admiral to keep these ships in sight. A half-hour later, the *Iris* signaled that they were the French fleet. The admiral at once gave the signal to form in line and make all sail. He overtook the French, and the engagement began at twelve-thirty. It lasted two hours until the French retired. The English did not follow, but instead, entered the Chesapeake.

Mar. 28 - The French fleet has returned to Rhode

Island. Their loss in the action on the sixteenth is not certain. That of the English is eighty dead and wounded. The French say that their undertaking in the Chesapeake Bay against General Arnold was betrayed, and claim that although they retired, they were prepared at all times to renew the action if Arbuthnot so desired. They would have done so anyway, if several of their ships had not been so heavily damaged, among which, especially, were *Conquerant* and *Ardent*, which had received fire from three English ships, and *Romulus*, which had opposed the English admiral's ship, would have been either sunk or captured if it had not been saved by special circumstances. Notation: This special circumstance to which the French refer is: Admiral Graves in the *London* wanted to break the enemy line. The *Romulus* opposed him. He, therefore, engaged it and would have certainly sunk it, but would have had to come out of the line. Therefore, Admiral Arbuthnot signaled him to remain in line, and as he did not execute at once, Admiral Arbuthnot fired several shots into the *London*. This brought on a quarrel between the two admirals, and is said to be the reason why the enemy was not pursued. The admiral, therefore, was blamed for having wasted the best opportunity for completely destroying the French fleet.

Apr. 5 - A post rider from the enemy headquarters to Philadelphia on May 29 was captured in the Jerseys

Jaeger Corps Journal

by some loyalists. Many interesting letters were found. One, from General Washington to his relatives in Virginia, of March 23, had the following paragraph:

By chance, we have heard nothing more of the two fleets since they left their respective harbors. We impatiently await news from the Chesapeake--God grant that it is good. It was bad. But, from the time I first suggested the destruction of Arnold, I had suspected that nothing would be undertaken by the French fleet and the troops on board, until after the English fleet left the English harbor. Therefore, only a small squadron was sent, which only took the *Romulus*, and could, as I had expected, take no action against Portsmouth without land troops.

Apr. 7 - A newspaper from Philadelphia provided the news that Lord Cornwallis has won an important victory over General Greene near Guilford, on the border of Virginia. General Greene's report of this affair:

Ironworks--March 16, 1781 - The army marched from High Rock Fort on March 12 and arrived on the fourteenth at Guilford Courthouse. The enemy lay near the Quaker Meeting on Deep River, eight miles away. On the morning of the fifteenth, our patrols discovered the enemy approaching on the Great Salisbury Road. The army moved forward in three lines. The first consisted of the North Carolina militia, under General [John] Butler; the second of the

Jaeger Corps Journal

Virginia militia, under General [Edward] Stephans; and the third of two brigades of Virginia and Maryland Continental troops, under General [Isaac] Huger, Colonel [William Augustine] Washington, with the dragoons, a detachment of light infantry, and one regiment of riflemen, which formed an observation corps on our right, and Lieutenant Colonel Lee, a similar corps on our left flank. The first line with two field cannon extended from the edge of a woods, behind fences which extended across its front. The second line was in a woods about an equal distance from it, so that it was three hundred yards behind the first, and the Continentals were an equal distance behind the second line, formed with a double front, because the rise on both wings was exposed to open fields. In this position, we awaited the enemy's arrival. After having sent our baggage to the rear in case of misfortune, Colonel Lee advanced against the enemy and had a vigorous skirmish with the advance troops. The action began with a twenty minute cannonade, after which the enemy advanced across the field with three columns: the Hessians on the right, the Guards in the middle, and Webster's Brigade on the left, in order to attack the North Carolinians. These awaited the attack until the enemy was within about 140 yards, when part of the North Carolinians fired, but a great number ran away without firing a shot. The generals and staff officers did everything possible to get the troops to make a stand, but neither the advantageous position nor any inducement could hold them back. The Virginia militia received the enemy with a warm and continuous firing for a long time. Then they were beaten back and the action became general. The observation corps was heavily engaged and above all, the battle was long and bitter, and the enemy only accomplished his mission because of his better discipline. The enemy scattered the Maryland Regiment, and our left wing was turned. Also, our Virginians fell back and our right appeared ready to crumble. I thought it was time to retreat and we retired in good order to Ready Fork River, crossing at the ford three miles from the battlefield. We then formed our troops and again assembled most of the troops which had been missing. We lost our artillery and two ammunition wagons. Major Anderson was killed, and Generals Huger and Stephans have been wounded. [End of Greene's report.]

Apr. 10 - General Philipps arrived in Virginia and has taken command of the troops there. On March 19, Captain Ewald was attacked by a reconnaisance force of five hundred men under Major General [Peter] Muhlenberg, which was beaten back after a very heavy engagement. During the morning, he sent a patrol forward consisting of one non-commissioned officer and six men to strengthen his outpost. They encountered the enemy marching toward them, fired, and were overtaken during their retreat. One man was killed, one wounded, and four captured. Only the non-commissioned officer was able to hide and escape. Shortly thereafter, the enemy attacked a picket of one non-commissioned officer and sixteen men, which was posted at a small dam. Captain Ewald hurried to their aid with nineteen men, defended the post for a considerable time, but was wounded, and Lieutenant Bickell took over the command, which exchanged fire with the enemy until they pulled back for an unknown reason. The Jaegers had one dead and one wounded. The rebels, 29 dead and wounded.

Apr. 18 - Admiral Arbuthnot returned to New York with the fleet from Virginia.

Apr. 29 - The two Ansbach regiments and the 43rd and 17th Infantry Regiments were embarked in order to go to Virginia. The fleet convoyed them.

Jaeger Corps Journal

May 4 - The French fleet has made no movement from Rhode Island. A camp has been established at Peekskill for their troops and General Wayne has made preparations to strengthen the troops in Virginia with 1,200 men. The rebel frigate *Confederacy*, of 36 guns, was captured, as well as some other ships under her convoy, and brought into New York. They were coming from Port o' Prince and destined for Philadelphia.

May 5 - Today the dispatches from Lord Cornwallis about the action at Guilford Courthouse arrived. They had been written on the battlefield, however, and contained no particulars except that he would pull back to Cape Fear River in order to retrieve his baggage, and especially provisions.

The light troops, before arriving at Guilford had been engaged with the enemy near Weitzel's Mill and had chased them away. In that action the Jaeger detachment suffered three dead and five wounded.

May 5 - The rebel frigate *Prostor*, of 26 guns, was captured.

Yesterday a party of rebels landed at Huntington Point in order to attack a party of Loyalists fortified at that place, but for unknown reasons, pulled back.

May 15 - Both armies still remain quiet. Only the Loyalists and the enemy skirmishers carry on the war in this region. Often, heated and bitter exchanges take place between the opposing forces, and more than

Jaeger Corps Journal

gruesome occurrences are more than occasionally perpetrated. The resulting plundering is always attributed to other nations by the armies' accounts.

May 18 - General Phillips occupies Petersburg on May 9. He embarked on April 18 at Portsmouth, with a party of the 76th and 80th Regiments, the Rangers, sixty jaegers, and Arnold's Legion. On the nineteenth he went up the James River to Burrel's Ferry. On the twentieth, Colonel Abercromby went up the Chickahominy with the Light Infantry. Colonel [John Graves] Simcoe, however, took a detachment to York, and Colonel Dundas landed at the mouth of the river. Generals Philipps and Arnold landed with the rest at Williamsburg. On the 22nd the troops marched to Chickahominy. Dundas joined them about five o'clock in the afternoon, and after the troops were again embarked, Abercromby also rejoined them the next morning. He had been twelve miles inland and had destroyed several ships, magazines, and such. At noon the fleet raised anchor and sailed up the James River to City Point, where a landing was made on the evening of the 24th. On the 25th the troops marched toward Petersburg, and arrived there at five o'clock in the evening. They were stopped about one mile from the city by a corps of militiamen under General Muhlenberg. They attacked the militia, who fled across the bridge, which they then destroyed, but experienced further pursuit, and lost about 100 men,

Jaeger Corps Journal

dead and wounded. The English had one dead and ten wounded.

On the 26th, the troops destroyed much tobacco, a number of ships, and the shipyard. On the 27th, General Philipps with the Light Infantry, a part of the Rangers, the Cavalry, and the Jaegers, marched to Chesterfield Courthouse, where he burned the enemy barracks for three hundred men. The same day General Arnold went with the rest of the troops to Osborn, where he arrived at noon. Four miles beyond Osborn lay a number of enemy ships, and as they would not surrender, he brought four cannon to bear against them. Although the ships lay down a heavy cannon fire, nevertheless Arnold's pieces, and especially the rifle fire of the Jaegers, had such a good effect, that all the ships surrendered. Two ships, three brigs, five sloops, and two schooners were captured, while many others were set on fire prior to the enemy abandoning them. Arnold had no boats with which to take immediate possession of them. At five o'clock in the evening, General Philipps joined Arnold, and after the boats arrived on the 29th, all the troops went up the river to Warwick. On the 30th, the troops marched to Manchester. The Marquis de Lafayette had arrived at Richmond the day before, and had drawn the militia under [Friedrich Wilhelm von] Steuben and Muhlenberg to him. As Richmond lies just opposite Manchester and is only separated by the river, he was

Jaeger Corps Journal

a witness to the smoke rising from the magazines set afire by the English. The same evening the troops returned to Warwick, and there destroyed a flour storage center and several beautiful mills. From the first to the sixth, troops returned to Hoyesland. On the seventh they again went up the river and landed at Brandon. On the ninth the Light Infantry and a part of the Rangers went to City Point in boats, and the rest of the troops marched to Petersburg, where they arrived that night, after a long march. As the troops left Bermuda Hundred, Lafayette marched to Williamsburg by means of a forced march via Long Bridge, over the Chickahominy River. Therefore, the fleet returned to Brandon and by means of this maneuver forced the Marquis, as quickly as possible, once again to turn back. He arrived at Osborn on the eighth and planned to cross near Petersburg, but just then the English troops unexpectedly met him and made several officers, who were to have obtained boats for the army in Petersburg, prisoners. Therefore, Lafayette returned to Richmond.

May 19 - General Philipps is reportedly deadly sick. Lieutenant General [James] Robertson therefore, went in a frigate to the Chesapeake today, in order to assume command of the troops there.

May 20 - Through the chief quartermaster's orders, we learned that Lord Rawdon had defeated General Greene with 1,400 Continentals, and a corps

Jaeger Corps Journal

of militia near Camden on April 19. After the affair at Guilford, and as Lord Cornwall had gone to the Cape Fear River, Greene took his best troops and cavalry in order once again to fall on South Carolina, and arrived at Camden after a march of eighty miles. He planned to overrun the posts in that area, but luck was not with him. Lord Rawdon marched with a far bigger force from Camden, and attacked him in his camp on Hobkirk's Hill

May 21 - This evening at seven o'clock, the Jaeger Corps received orders to march to Jamaica immediately, or as soon as possible, taking all baggage along, and there to await further orders.

May 22 - We broke camp this night, and at nine o'clock in the morning were in Jamaica. At noon we received orders once again to march back to our quarters. There had been a report that the enemy's war chest would cross the North River under a strong escort, but it was groundless.

May 28 - Lieutenant General Robertson, who had gone to Virginia a short time ago to assume command of the troops at that place, returned today with the report that General Philipps had died on the fifteenth, and that Lord Cornwallis with his troops, had joined those at Petersburg, and had taken over command. Therefore, his army presently consists of the Guards, Light Infantry, the 17th Foot, 23rd, 33rd, 43rd, 71st, 76th, and 80th Regiments, the Hereditary Prince, Bose, and

Jaeger Corps Journal

Ansbach Regiments, a detachment of Jaegers under Ewald (because the detachment under Captain Roeder had been left on the Cape Fear River), the Queen's Rangers, the British Legion, the American Legion, and the Loyal Americans.

June 10 - The American Legion and the Loyal Americans returned to New York with General Arnold, from Virginia.

June 11 - The following troops received orders to camp on York Island and Long Island: 17th Dragoons, Grenadiers, 38th and 42nd Regiments, and Jaegers, Leib and Young Lossberg Regiments, the Combined Battalion, 3rd Battalion of Delancy's, and 4th Battalion of Skinner's Provincials, and the Loyal Americans.

June 12 - From the West Indies we hear that a French fleet of 22 ships of the line, under Comte de Grasse arrived at Martinique, and that Admiral Hood, who had been before that harbor with fifteen ships, found it necessary to fight his way through the French, which he did with few casualties. This affair occurred on April 16. Hood sailed to St. Lucia, and detached the *Russell* to Eustacia to inform Admiral Rodney of the event.

June 13 - Admiral Arbuthnot is cruising with his fleet off Rhode Island. Mr. de Barras must have had an expedition planned. He had 1,200 men on board and wanted to sail out, but Arbuthnot was visible, and the troops were again debarked.

Jaeger Corps Journal

June 16 - Today the army began to go into camp. Lieutenant Colonel von Wurmb remained with the Jaeger Corps and the 17th Dragoon Regiment on Long Island, in order to provide cover. He took his first camp at Buckenem, and changed it several times in order to insure grazing for the cavalry horses.

June 23 - The enemy army had moved some time ago, and the French have marched out from Rhode Island. Lieutenant Colonel von Wurmb, therefore, received orders toward the end of the month to leave Long Island, and to cross over to the army on York Island.

Brigadier General Skinner went with a detachment (including one hundred jaegers under Captain Hinrichs) to Middleton in the Jerseys to drive in cattle. The expedition however, did not accomplish what one would have expected. The Jaegers had a skirmish with the militia and were not supported. Otherwise, they could have captured the entire body. The Jaegers lost two men. Only about forty head of cattle represented the complete conquest.

June 28 - The Jaegers and Dragoons today left their camp near Cool Spring, and marched to Jamaica. The Jaegers then went to Kingsbridge over Hell Gate, and the Dragoon Regiment remained at Flushing.

July 2 - Lieutenant Colonel von Wurmb today went over Kingsbridge to the Plains, in order to collect information about the enemy and his movements. On

Jaeger Corps Journal

his return from Baboeks to Philipse's House, he encountered an enemy ambush of thirty men, whose advance post of five men opened fire, fatally wounding Captain [Carl] von Rau, in the breast. The Cavalry at once charged the rebels, capturing the first five, but the detachment was able to save itself because of the denseness of the trees. A cavalryman and a horse were killed in the engagement.

July 3 - This evening, at nine o'clock Lieutenant Colonel Emmerich with one hundred men went to Philipse's House to lay in ambush. The next morning, two hundred jaegers were to move out as an escort for the hay wagons being sent out. During the night, at twelve o'clock, the news was brought to Lieutenant Colonel von Wurmb that the enemy army was marching, and that the enemy's advance troops had been seen at Sing Sing. The wagons therefore, were ordered back, and Lieutenant Colonel von Prueschenck was then ordered to march to Philipse's with two hundred jaegers and thirsty cavalry, in order to gather more detailed information, and especially to cover the withdrawal of Lieutenant Colonel Emmerich. He marched at daybreak, and had barely passed Kingsbridge when he heard firing near Philipse's. He therefore marched rapidly, and although he also had spoken with a patrol sent from the bridge defenses every hour, to the opposite line at Fort Independence, which had reported to him that

Jaeger Corps Journal

everything was secure, he nevertheless used the saving precaution to detach a non-commissioned officer and ten men to visit this old fort, before he passed the defile line close by the foot of the hills, and between the Harlem Creek. This small party discovered the enemy which had lain in ambush in the fort, and which must have just arrived. First, the Jaegers believed it to be Lieutenant Colonel Emmerich, until the enemy opened fire. Lieutenant [Johann] Schaeffer, who with the advance guard in the meantime, had already entered the defile and therefore was cut off from the lieutenant colonel, received the enemy fire at close range, retreated into the swamp through which he was able to work his way, and rejoined the Corp. However, in so doing, he lost several men. The lieutenant colonel thereupon made a spirited attack on the fort, but because the narrowness of the terrain seriously hindered him, his infantry could not spread out enough, and began to draw together. Therefore, he tried in this necessity, to cut through with the cavalry under Lieutenant Flies. This also was repulsed.

Jaeger Corps Journal

Meanwhile, however, he was able to chase the enemy into the fort, which gave his infantry time, according to his purpose, to somewhat regroup and to win more and better terrain. By moving to the right, he gained an advantage, enabling him to seize an old house from which he could attack the enemy more advantageous. Eventually he drove the enemy from the fort and was able to occupy it. The entire Corps meanwhile crossed over the bridge, and joined with the lieutenant colonel in the fort. The enemy marched onto the opposite height (about a distance of one thousand paces) and could have consisted of six or seven hundred men. The lieutenant's colonel's advance guard under Captain Hinrichs continued firing. Meantime, Emmerich and his detachment had retired across the Spiting Devil, and was separated from us by the river, because the enemy had occupied the bridge over the river. Therefore, it was necessary to drive the enemy from this position. Lieutenant Colonel von Wurmb pressed forward with this intent with the entire Corps--the Cavalry on the right wing. The enemy did not retire in panic, but pulled back slowly, holding off the attackers. Our flankers meantime pushed forward under a continuous fire. After the bridge was cleared and Emmerich again had use of it, Lieutenant Colonel von Wurmb halted, as moments before he had received a report from a loyalist sent to him, that the enemy cavalry was posted

Jaeger Corps Journal

on the Williamsbridge. The enemy maneuver closed that route leading to Devanas' house and so, if the Jaegers were followed, would expose our right flank on an open stretch of terrain, where the enemy cavalry could attack without any hindrance. Emmerich then rejoined the Corps and reported the approach of the enemy army. An enemy patrol had run into him, and of this patrol he had killed several and taken three prisoners, but was then compelled to retreat down the North River, crossing at Spiting Devil to prevent his being cut off. Lieutenant Colonel von Wurmb decided not to challenge the enemy, who had far more infantry than he had, as well as three hundred cavalry, and were in his rear. So he took post in the fort and sent his report to headquarters. Toward three o'clock an enemy column came over Valentine's Hill and detached a brigade to Spiting Devil over Cordland's Reach. At this the Jaeger Corps left the fort, and took a position on the heights on the other side of Kingsbridge. However, Captain von Wangheim had to remain in the fort with one hundred men. The enemy general staff reconnoitered the Spiting Devil before our defenses and the enemy army, toward four o'clock, moved into a camp on Valentine's Hill over Cordland's Reach to Spiting Devil, whereupon the Jaeger Corps marched back on a line with the bridges to its former camp. Our losses in today's affair were three men dead and one officer and twenty men wounded. On the other hand, the enemy losses, according to subsequent reports, amounted to one hundred dead and wounded. Colonel [Alexander] Scammel had been engaged with Lieutenant Colonel von Prueschenck, and his troops had consisted of a regiment of light infantry and four hundred men of General Washington's Guard.

July 4 - The commanding general made known his special recognition of Lieutenant Colonel von Wurmb and Lieutenant Colonel von Prueschenck for their roles in yesterday's affair.

This afternoon, the enemy army marched back and set up camp at White Plains. Captain von Rau died of his wounds today.

July 7 - The French troops under [Jean Baptiste Donatien de Vimeur, Comte de] Rochambeau joined with those of General Washington. They consisted of the Regiments of Bourbonnois, Soissonois, Santonge, and Royal Du Pont, the Legion of Lauzun, and Artillery, in all, four thousand men and three hundred horses. The rebel army consists of about nine thousand men. The French are on the left wing, and according to all reports, the object of their operations is New York, but this must be held in abeyance until their fleet arrives from the West Indies.

July 8 - News from the West Indies is that on May 11, the French appeared before St. Lucia with 25 ships of the line and landed two thousand men, in order to retake the island. However, they took the men back aboard ship on the thirteenth without having undertaken further action. They then sailed to Tobago and captured that small island. Admiral Rodney sailed with his fleet to St. Lucia expecting to encounter the French there. They had departed however, so he sailed to Tobago, but arrived too late.

July 9 - Don [Bernardo] Galvez has captured Pensacola. He besieged it with twenty thousand men for nine weeks, and the English garrison, consisting of 1,100 men, surrendered and are not to serve again against Spain or France. No notice was taken of the rebels. A part of these troops arrived in New York, as well as their commander, Lieutenant General [John] Campbell.

July 10 - Lord Cornwallis and his army are at Williamsburg.

An affair occurred between Lieutenant Colonel Simcoe and the enemy during the march, in which four officers and sixteen men of the enemy were captured, although their force was more than twice as strong. During this engagement, Simcoe commanded the Cavalry, and Captain Ewald commanded the Jaegers and Rangers, who were on foot. Both commanders were thanked in orders by Lord Cornwallis.

July 12 - Two French frigates have been seen in the [Long Island] Sound, in order to capture the ships

Jaeger Corps Journal

carrying wood for the loyalists. For the most part however, these ships saved themselves. Therefore, the French debarked their marines, and they marched against the loyalists' post at Lloyd's Neck. They retreated after receiving some cannon shots, which killed some French.

June 16 - As the enemy has laid out some defenses at Dobb's Ferry and brought his provisions to the North River at Tarrytown, several armed ships sailed up the river today and captured two rebel sloops with eight hundred barrels of flour, which deprived the enemy of bread for three days. The enemy defenses fired at the ships, but did them little damage, although they anchored in the Tappan Sea.

July 17 - Marquis de Lafayette attacked Lord Cornwallis near Portsmouth in Virginia, on July 6, as he was crossing a river, but was defeated and had to leave behind three cannon, and three hundred dead and wounded. He had a strength of three thousand men and believed most of the army had crossed the river, and that he would engage with only the rear guard. He found himself in error however, as the Lord had heard of his approach and had lain in wait for him.

July 18 - Some loyalists today killed a French hussar riding master. They had lain in ambush near the French pickets, and he had been riding with a seven-man patrol.

July 19 - The armed ships which had lain at

Jaeger Corps Journal

Tappan Sea re-passed Dobb's Ferry, from which they received a heavy cannonade and lost fourteen men. This morning at daybreak, the enemy army appeared on the Heights of Fordham and went into camp there. At nine o'clock, an enemy party attacked Frog's Neck and plundered the loyalist post at that place. The loyalists themselves, after a brief resistance, entered their boats and left the area. Morrisiana, deserted by the loyalists, was plundered by two regiments, and several cannons shots were exchanged between the enemy and our Redoubt No. 8. The Jaeger Corps was harassed by the enemy artillery fire, and therefore broke camp and brought their baggage back within the lines, in order to protect it in the event of an enemy attack. Several cannon shots were directed at our Cavalry, but no harm was done. The Jaeger Corps lay under arms throughout the entire night and strengthened all its pickets along the Harlem Creek, and at the Charles Redoubt (on the head of land at Kingsbridge). No. 8 was also reinforced by the infantry.

July 22 - At two o'clock this afternoon the enemy army withdrew. Their left wing marched over Eastchester and the right wing over Miles Square. A French regiment and a rebel regiment constituted the rear guard, and did not leave Fort Independence until late at night.

July 24 - The enemy army has its camp at

Jaeger Corps Journal

Tuckahoe, the right wing at Dobb's Ferry, and the left over Tuckahoe as far as the Bronx River. The Legion of Lauzun is at White Plains, and General Smallwood, with the militia, is at the Sawpits.

In Carolina things are not going well. General Greene has occupied Camden and captured Augusta. Lord Rawdon has had to withdraw into all the English outer posts, and Greene now has Ninety-Six under siege.

July 25 - On the previous Sunday, a party of loyalists went from Lloyd's Neck to Middle Essex in New England, and surprised the local population at church services. Fifty men, as prisoners, and forty saddle horses were seized and brought back. A partisan raid in a civil war.

July 26 - Admiral Graves, who has now taken command of the fleet, went to sea today in order to cruise.

General Greene stormed Ninety-Six but was repulsed, and found it necessary to raise the siege, because reinforcements from Charleston (namely three regiments recently arrived from England) under Lord Rawdon were nearing the post.

Aug. 4 - From the packet boat we have learned that Mr. la Mottres Piquet has taken most of the St. Eustacia fleet off Seilly. Commodore Hotham was convoying it with four ships of the line, and took flight with the remainder toward Ireland.

Jaeger Corps Journal

Aug. 11 - Today the fleet with the German recruits arrived. They had sailed around Scotland and spent 93 days at sea. The men were exceedingly sickly.

The *Iris* captured the rebel frigate *Trumbull*, of 32-guns, off the Cape of Delaware.

The *Bellesaius,* of 24-guns, was also brought in by two of our frigates and various other enemy ships have recently been taken.

Aug. 18 - The enemy army is moving and crossing the North River. Everyone believes that Washington plans to attack New York, and will march toward Paulus Hook and Staten Island. At least General Clinton is of this opinion, although Lieutenant Colonel von Wurmb, who has permission to engage spies, gave the general a report that New York will not be attacked, but that Washington is marching to Virginia. This is based on two reasons: first, because the commissary has ordered forage and bread to be collected and ready as far as Trenton, and along the Delaware River; second, because an American woman, mistress of a distinguished French officer, was sent to Trenton, where she is to await the arrival of the army.

Aug. 29 - Yesterday Admiral Hood arrived at Sandy Hook from the West Indies with thirteen ships of the line.

The enemy army suddenly dropped the pretense and marched toward Trenton, crossing the Delaware there, and thus clearly showing the intention of going to Virginia.

Aug. 30 - Therefore, the greatest part of our army, including three hundred jaegers, was ordered to be prepared to embark.

Aug. 31 - The three hundred jaegers, under Lieutenant Colonel von Wurmb marched at three o'clock this morning, in order to embark from Kingsbridge. However, they were ordered back, and the entire embarkation was cancelled.

Sep. 1 - Admiral Graves sailed for the Chesapeake with the fleet, as the French are said to have already arrived there.

Sep. 3 - General Arnold, with one hundred jaegers under Captain von Wangenheim, the 40th, 54th, and 57th Regiments went by ship today to New England.

Sep. 4 - The following troops were ordered to embark on September 6: four hundred jaegers under Lieutenant Colonel von Wurmb, the 17th Dragoons, all the Grenadiers, the 42nd and 57th Regiments, and the Leib and Prince Charles Regiments.

Sep. 5 - The French fleet, with 26 ships of the line lies in the Chesapeake, and has blockaded Lord Cornwallis. Admiral Graves has only nineteen ships of the line, and two 50-gun ships. The frigate *Pegasus* has also sighted Mr. de Barras with eight ships of the line, as he is sailing from Rhode Island to the Chesapeake to unite with de Grasse.

Jaeger Corps Journal

Sep. 6 - The troops were embarked today aboard transport ships.

Sep. 7 - From the *Zebra,* sloop of war which arrived from England in seven weeks, we have learned that Commodore Johnston was attacked on May 1 in the Bay of St. Iago by a French squadron, which had been sent after him, but which was then defeated by him. A French ship had already struck its colors, but Captain Salton neglected to board it, so it saved itself. Johnston was bound for the Cape of Good Hope, but if he can now escape from the French, is at best doubtful.

Sep. 10 - General Arnold departed for New London, with his detachment at six o'clock, burned the city, stormed a fort, and captured the garrison of seventy men, whose colonel was killed, along with 22 men. The 40th and 54th Regiments which stormed the fort, lost many men. The rebels, although militia, defended themselves well. The ships in the harbor used the wind, which was against the English, to save themselves by sailing up the river. Those at the wharves however, were burned, and magazines of great value were destroyed. The fort was to have been blown up, and only in this were the orders not carried out.

Sep. 13 - This detachment returned. The Jaegers went on board at once, and the 22nd Regiment embarked, replacing the 54th Regiment, which had suffered many casualties.

This night a frigate arrived from the Chesapeake with the news that on the fifth an action had occurred between the two fleets, but without a decisive result. On the arrival of the English, the French had slipped their anchors, and sailed against the Englanders.

Sep. 15 - The transport ships sailed to The Narrows today.

Sep. 19 - This morning Admiral Graves returned with his fleet, and we at once noticed that the action on the fifth had not been the most fortunate one. Only twelve of our ships of the line had been engaged, the others had not fired a shot because our maneuvers had been so poorly directed.

At least the admiral has been blamed for making a great mistake, by letting the French ships sail out individually, without attacking them at once. From the fifth to the eleventh, both fleets maneuvered off Cape Henry. On the eleventh, the French returned to the Chesapeake where they joined together with Mr. de Barras, who had arrived there in the meantime, and unfortunately had captured two of our frigates, which had been sent in to cut off the French anchor buoys. Thereafter, Graves, with his nineteen ships of the line could no longer attack the French, and so decided to return to New York. Further, it became necessary on the thirteenth to burn the *Terrible*, of 74-guns, because it was very old and had been damaged greatly in the

Jaeger Corps Journal

action.

Sep. 20 - The embarked troops today went to Staten Island and were set on land. Our warship fleet went to New York in order to complete repairs there.

Sep. 25 - Admiral Digby arrived at Sandy Hook yesterday evening. He had Prince William Henry with him, but instead of the six expected ships of the line, he had only three--*Prince George, Canada,* and *Lion,* and one 50-gun ship.

An express boat came from Lord Cornwallis. He has still not come under siege. Washington however, has arrived at Head of Elk and is waiting for the French transport ships, which will take him to Virginia.

Sep. 28 - The warship fleet is too damaged to be repaired. The troops received orders to be prepared to go aboard the same. The army train has been assembled at Staten Island and many pontoons have been loaded on wagons, as if the army is to go into the Jerseys.

Jaeger Corps Journal

Oct. 2 - The Grenadiers and Jaegers marched to the south part of Staten Island and camped at Richmond, the Jaegers at Old Blazing Star. This movement makes a diversion into the Jerseys appear likely.

Oct. 7 - Yesterday, the Cork fleet arrived. It consisted of seventy sail.

Oct. 10 - Today the troops on Staten Island marched back to Cole's Ferry in order to board warships. This allowed the Jerseys to recover from the fear of a diversionary attack.

Oct. 11 - Two ships of the line arrived today from the West Indies.

Oct. 12 - After the troops passed in review before Prince William Henry, they embarked on board the transport ships.

Oct. 13 - A stormy southwest wind drove a warship against the *Shrewsbury*, losing its bowsprit. Several boats capsized in the fleet, causing some drowning.

Oct. 13 [sic] - We learned from the placket boat from England of an engagement in the Channel on August 5 between Commodore Steward and the Hollanders.

Oct. 14 - Most of the warships, except for the *Europa*, and the transport ships, sailed to Sandy Hook. The transports lay alongside of the warships, enabling the troops to cross from one to the other

Jaeger Corps Journal

across boards placed between ships. The Jaegers went aboard the *Lion*, of 64-guns (Lieutenant Colonel von Wurmb and 250 men) and on the *Europa*, of 74-guns, (Major von Wurmb and 150 men). The first is commanded by Captain Focks. It was a new ship, and the third of Admiral [Francis Samuel] Drake's division in the advance guard (on the star board tack).

After the embarkation, the warships crossed the bar and then dropped anchor.

Oct. 19 - After the war fleet had all crossed the bar, they set sail this afternoon at four o'clock with a weak southwest wind. There were 24 ships of the line, three 50-gun ships, and two fire ships. We passed the long awaited fleet from London, which however, had as warship only the *Renown*, of 50-guns, as an escort.

Oct. 20 - Strong southwest wind - the fleet sailed in three divisions (sailing order).

Oct. 21 - Wind southwest.

Oct. 22 - Winds as before., but not strong - the strength of a calm.

Oct. 23 - Wind southwest.

Oct. 24 - During the day the wind was southwesterly, at night northwesterly and very strong. We made various course changes with the entire fleet, during which the smartness and speed of ther maneuvering by the warships was worth watching.

Oct. 25 - We saw the Capes of Virginia. The day was bright and calm, the night wind northwesterly,

Jaeger Corps Journal

very strong. Therefore, we withdrew from the land, and remained out at sea.

Oct. 26 - Wind southwesterly, very strong during the day. At night northwesterly.

Oct. 27 - Wind northwesterly. We saw Cape Charles, and a French ship. The evening was calm.

Oct. 28 - Wind northwesterly. We saw Cape Henry and entered the bay. At four o'clock in the afternoon we saw the French fleet lying at anchor, ready to challenge our using the passage. Our fleet was in line (abreast) and lay to. The admiral sent on land for news. This he obtained, but to the effect that Lord Cornwallis had been captured. The wind was very favorable for the French to attack us whenever they wished.

Oct. 29 - Our fleet still lay as before. The French were peacefully at anchor. One of our frigates was sent to England with the unfortunate news. The day was still and beautiful, and at four o'clock in the afternoon the fleet set sail in a weak wind for New York. The French watched us from a distance from two frigates.

Oct. 30 - A good wind from the southwest. We lost sight of the French frigates.

Oct. 31 - Pleasant southerly wind.

Nov. 1 - Wind southeasterly with rain, high seas, and squalls.

Nov. 2 - The weather calmed. At eight o'clock in

Jaeger Corps Journal

the morning we saw Sandy Hook, and, as the wind was from the northwest, we anchored about four o'clock in the afternoon near the Hook.

Nov. 3 - At noon today, we went from the warships onto the transports, and were landed this evening at Denyce's Ferry. As the wind began to blow exceptionally hard from the northwest, however, we had to remain at anchor.

Nov. 4 - 12 - The northwesterly wind blew without the least change during the day, as well as during the night, so that it was impossible to land. Many ships exhausted the supply of provisions and water, but nothing could be done to help them because no boats could be lowered. Meantime we tried to run in, to no avail, and continued to lose ground where we were anchored.

Nov. 13 - Today the ships finally entered The Narrows, as the wind had eased. The troops debarked, part at Denyse's Ferry, and part into the already arranged winter quarters in New York. The Jaegers debarked at Denyse's Ferry and marched into the previous year's winter quarters at Westbury, Jericho, and Herricks on Long Island.

Nov. 14 - The French and Americans were very thorough in planning the works necessary for the siege of Lord Cornwallis. Initially, they began on September 30 with the approaches, and on October 6, their first parallel was completed at a distance of only

Jaeger Corps Journal

six hundred yards from the English defenses. During the evening of October 9, they opened batteries and soon silenced the English with their ceaseless bombardment. During the night of October 11, they began their second parallel, and on the evening of the fourteenth, stormed and conquered two redoubts commanded by Major Campbell, which protected the English. These were absorbed into the second parallel, upon which the French worked untiringly, during the same night. Lord Cornwallis saw that when the cannon in the second parallel opened fire, he would not be able to withstand it, as his defenses were too weak. He made a sortie therefore, before daybreak on October 16, with 320 men commanded by Colonel Abercromby, and spiked eleven cannon. This did not help much however, because they were soon bored out, and by evening the parallel was completed. Lord Cornwallis was convinced the post could no longer be defended and decided to cross over with most of the troops to Gloucester where his light troops were being blockaded by a French corps), and try to proceed to New York by land from there, as he planned to overcome the French corps. He had already sent over part of his troops in sixteen boats when, in that same night, a dreadful wind storm arose which prevented his continuing the operation. Next morning he brought them back across, and the French opened fire with their batteries at daybreak, so

Jaeger Corps Journal

destroying the English defenses that they could have been stormed when the French so desired. Lord Cornwallis therefore decided to capitulate.

On October 19, the capitulation was signed by which he and his troops surrendered under the same terms as accorded at Charleston. Cornwallis says: York was meant to be only a fortified camp. He had only begun work there on August 1, and he had had only four hundred pieces of engineering equipment. He would never have chosen this position if he had not been ordered to do so. From the beginning, when Washington came to Williamsburg with his army, he would have sought either to engage the enemy on an open field, or to proceed to New York by land, if he had not received firm assurances from Sir Henry Clinton of a reinforcement which kept him from the choice of these desperate measures. Finally, he had received a letter of September 24, assuring him that the fleet with reinforcements would sail on October 5.

Nov. 15 - Admiral Graves sailed for the West Indies with a fleet of nineteen ships of the line on November 11, because the French fleet had already sailed on the third. Four French ships of the line are lying in the Chesapeake. The French troops are improving the defenses of Yorktown, and are commanded by Rochambeau. A part of the rebel army is on the move to Philadelphia to go into winter quarters. Another part, however, has gone south to

Jaeger Corps Journal

strengthen General Greene, who is situated not far from Charleston. Wilmington has been abandoned and all the posts in South Carolina have been pulled to within a few miles of Charleston. The rebel army is wintering at Morristown. This is one of the most peaceful winter quarters of the entire war. Neither army has undertaken any activity, as if the surrender at Yorktown has already brought an end to everything.

St. Eustacia has been overrun by the Marquis de Bouville, and conquered by two hundred men, although Colonel Cockburn had occupied the island with six hundred men. (October 25).

We have also lost St. Kitts. The French placed it under siege and conquered it on February 26. Admiral Hood had two engagements with the French, neither being decisive, and he arrived a short time later with twelve ships of the line, but the French had already sailed to Martinique.

Jaeger Corps Journal
1782

Mar. 30 - By today's orders the army was divided into brigades, and the generals assigned specific districts in which they are to command. Lieutenant Colonel von Wurmb was named inspector general of all the Cavalry, and Captain Metzner was made brigade-major. Therefore, the Dragoon Regiment of Lieutenant Colonel Thomson was ordered to march from Staten Island to the fresh meadows east of Jamaica, and make camp there.

Apr. 27 - The packet boat brought us the unpleasant news that Fort St. Philips on the Island of Minorca had been surrendered by General Murray to the Duc de Crillon on February 12, and that Parliament had voted against an offensive war with America. Also, that General Clinton is to return home, and General [Sir Guy] Carleton will assume command. Of no less importance, Lieutenant General von Knyphausen, at his request, is to return home, and Lieutenant General [Friedrich Wilhelm, Freiherr] von Lossberg will assume command of the Hessian troops.

May 1 - The army received orders to take no manner of offensive movement without the express approval of the commanding general.

The army exercises therefore, and since there is nothing else to do, exercises very diligently.

May 5 - General Carleton arrived in New York on the *Zeres* frigate, and brought the noteworthy news

Jaeger Corps Journal

that the King has changed ministers, and accepted the opposition party.

May 9 - Lieutenant General von Lossberg assumed command of the Hessians.

May 10 - Sir Guy Carleton took over command of the army.

May 11 - A ship which arrived from St. Johns has brought the good news of the sea battle on April 12 between Admiral Rodney and Comte de Grasse, in which the latter, with the *Ville de Paris*, of 110-guns, and three other ships of the line were captured, one sunk, and one, which had already struck, blew up.

This battle saved the Island of Jamaica, and otherwise, the French would have united with the Spanish and put the island under siege, and in all probability, would have captured it.

May 21 - Today the army passed in review before Sir Guy Carleton.

June 10 - Lieutenant Colonel von Wurmb camped with the Cavalry of the army and the Jaeger Corps at various locations on Long Island, not only to protect the island from the frequent plundering raids from New England, but also, so the horses could have grazing.

June 12 - The army broke quarters, and camped within the lines on York Island.

The enemy is encamped at Verplanck's Point, and absolutely quiet.

Jaeger Corps Journal

July 3 - The economy orders which have been in preparation for a considerable period of time appeared in orders today. All company wagons and horses, all surplus shipping, and all forage for captains [and all junior officers?] has been cut off. Rations for staff officers have been reduced, and above all, many unnecessary commissaries and departments eliminated, and thereby there is really a great savings.

July 22 - The Cork provisions fleet arrived.

July 24 - Lieutenant Colonel von Wurmb marched with his corps into camp at Flushing.

Aug. 3 - As we have received reports that the French fleet returning from the West Indies was seen not far from Sandy Hook, and it is to be feared that it will attack New York, Admiral [Robert] Digby anchored all the armed ships on the other side of the bar, and by an express, the Jaeger Corps received orders to march immediately to Denyse's Ferry to protect the coast and the landing areas there. Here we met Colonel [Gabriel] Ludlow's Brigade, consisting of four provincial regiments, and which were joined with the Jaegers, all under the command of Colonel von Wurmb, and all of whom were then camped in various locations.

Aug. 25 - Definite reports came in that the French fleet has sailed for Boston, and that Admiral [Hugh] Pigot, who had replaced Admiral Rodney in the West Indies, is expected here at any moment. The

Jaeger Corps Journal

threatening danger has thus passed, and the army has been ordered to move into a formal camp on York Island. Therefore, on August 26, the Jaegers marched to Morris Hill.

Sep. 6 - Today Admiral Pigot arrived at Sandy Hook with 26 ships of the line. The army is camped in three lines at McGowan's Pass, seven miles from New York.

1st Line - under Brigadier General Musgrave - English Grenadiers and the 38th Regiment.

2nd Line - under Lieutenant General Campbell - 7th, 37th, 42nd, and 54th Regiments, Leib and Prince Charles Regiments.

3rd Line - under Colonel von Wurmb - Jaegers, 17th Dragoons, the Hesse Hanauers.

The Hessian Grenadiers and regiments have not yet been united with these troops, but have orders to march. There is a great shortage of water in the camp, and the regiments and corps must dig wells. Due to a shortage, the Jaegers have borrowed tents from the English depot.

Charleston, just like Savannah, which was vacated on July 15, is to be abandoned, according to the general discussion, which is accepted as true by everyone. The troops in Savannah all went to St. Augustine, except for the 7th and Knoblauch Regiments, which arrived on August 15 at Sandy Hook.

Jaeger Corps Journal

Sep. 15 - Colonel von Wurmb with the reserve corps and the English Grenadiers made a general foraging movement as far as Eastchester. Major General [Friedrich Wilhelm] von Wurmb's Brigade pushed forward to the other side of Kingsbridge as a support force, to be on hand in case of an attack, but everything remained quiet

Sep. 23 - Today the Hessian Grenadiers and the Landgraf, Knyphausen, and Buenau Regiments marched into the first and second lines in the camp. Lieutenant General von Lossberg now commands the second line.

The army has set its pickets at regular and measured distances, as if facing the enemy. A brigadier, two staff officers, and a brigade-major are named to duty daily.

Sep. 24 - All officers and men assigned to the regiments in the southern provinces were embarked today in order to go to their units.

Oct. 4 - The army moved out today in order to pass in review before the commanding general. The first and second lines marched to Morris House in two columns. For each of these, the reserve corps provided the light troops to serve as an advance guard. The reserve corps itself marched to Harlem Plain, where it alone passed in review, and after having done so, the army marched in the designated order back into camp again.

Jaeger Corps Journal

Oct. 13 - As the German recruits who arrived in Halifax in August no longer will be coming here to their regiments, it was decided today that their money and equipment should be sent to them. Also, officers and non-commissioned officers are to go there to drill them. Lieutenant [Franz Georg] Bauer of the Jaeger Corps is among those being sent.

Oct 28 - Winter quarters for the army were designated in today's orders. Many regiments marched at once into theirs. The reserve corps however, marched to Morris Hill to be organized into foraging units, which daily will consist of two hundred men and fifty horses.

Nov. 3 - All troops except the reserve vacated their camps today, and went into quarters.

Nov. 12 - After all the forage was brought in, the reserve broke camp today, went across the East River at Hell Gate, and entered winter quarters at Westbury, Jericho, Oyster Bay, Herrichs, and Hampstadt. Lieutenant Colonel Thomson, with his Dragoon Regiment, the Legion, and the Queen's Rangers had already entered Huntington, and had to provide his own defenses.

Nov. 15 - Admiral Pigot, after sending various ships to England, sailed with the rest to the West Indies. The French had up till this time, lain in Boston, peaceful and undisturbed, with twelve ships, and have now followed after Admiral Pigot.

Jaeger Corps Journal

Dec. 17 - The merchant fleet sailed for England, taking all the invalids and other people who otherwise are attached to the army, who either belong to destroyed corps, were incapable of performing duty, or who, according to the new economic plan, can no longer be employed, or were prisoners of war, so that throughout the army a large number of useless people have departed, and seen in retrospect, provide a savings on provisions, wood, etc.

Dec. 25 - The New Englanders had planned to attack Lieutenant Colonel Thomson in Huntington, and had collected the necessary boats at Stanford. We received timely reports, and therefore each night a strong jaeger detachment was sent to Cool Springs to cut off the enemy's retreat, when he actually attacked Huntington. This occurred five days in a row. As always, this was also reported to the enemy, and he gave up his plan.

Jaeger Corps Journal

1783

Jan. 6 - The fleet with the garrison from Charleston arrived in New York. They had a quick and good passage.

The Jaeger Corps and the Hesse-Hanauers had to make a place for their quarters, and therefore, on the 7th, are to march to Huntington and Oyster Bay, where they will be quartered. Thomson's Dragoons, the Legion, and Rangers were in the barracks which Thomson had built, and at the same time fortified. The Hessian Jaegers were in the city, beside a detachment from the Ansbach Regiment. The Ansbach Jaeger Corps was at Norwich, and the Hesse-Hanau Corps at Oyster Bay. This district, as far as the east end of the island, was under the command of Colonel von Wurmb, and from which he allowed the collection of forage for the subsistence of the Cavalry, and at the same time, as all civilian government had been superceded, he had to settle all arguments between the inhabitants.

Feb. 12 - The Dragoon Regiment of Thomson, as well as part of the Jaegers, were sent to Jamaica due to a shortage of forage. In their place, the 1st Battalion of Delancy's Provincials came to Huntington. The New Englanders occasionally make small raids on the seacoast, otherwise nothing of note occurs, and in addition, the trade with New England for provisions is greatly encouraged, and fresh food-stuffs for the

Jaeger Corps Journal

subsistence of the army is brought over, as Huntington is most conveniently located.

Apr. 7 - Today the packet boat arrived in New York, and brought the armistice and the Articles of Parliament. The armistice was then formally proclaimed in New York on the eighth.

Apr. 11 - All the troops under Colonel von Wurmb were assembled today to formally hear the armistice. Broadsides were then sent to New England, and the inhabitants on Long Island likewise were made aware.

May 29 - At the request of Colonel von Wurmb, both the Jaeger Corps and the Hesse-Hanauers marched today to York Island, and entered the barracks at McGowan's Pass, because since the declaration of peace, desertions had become so frequent and the situation in this place is such that despite all efforts, nothing could be done to prevent them. The English troops remained in Huntington.

June 2 - Today embarkation lists for all the German troops were published and all possible preparations made for leaving America. The loyalists embarked therefore, in hoards, for Nova Scotia, the designated place of refuge. The Americans have also already reduced their army, which was very small before this action.

July 9 - A part of the Hanau Free Corps was embarked today.

July 15 - The rest of this corps went on board

Jaeger Corps Journal

today.

July 25 - The troops of Ansbach, Waldeck, and Zerbst were embarked.

Aug. 1 - Today the army entered a camp near Newton, on Long Island.

Aug. 4 - The Ditfurth, Knyphausen, Hereditary Prince, Bose, D'Angellelli, Knoblauch, Benning, and Buenaru Regiments received orders to be prepared to embark.

Aug. 12 & 13 - The above regiments embarked.

Sep. 9 - The provincial troops embarked for Nova Scotia.

Oct. 7 - The 37th and 44th Regiments did the same.

Oct. 21 - Colonel von Wurmb today assumed command over the posts at Kingsbridge and McGowan's Pass. At the first, the 38th and 80th Regiments are stationed.

Oct. 25 - Today the Grenadier Battalion Platte marched into the barracks near the Jaegers at McGowan's Pass.

Nov. 11 - The 38th Regiment marched into garrison at New York.

Nov. 21 - Today the rest of the Hessian troops and the 80th Regiment embarked. The 80th Regiment had been at Kingsbridge, and as an appointment had been made with General Washington to hand over that post, and the one at McGowan's Pass, today. Colonel von Wurmb had been instructed to leave the post at eight

Jaeger Corps Journal

o'clock in the morning, as soon as the Americans arrived. At seven o'clock, the regiment was prepared to march out, and as soon as the American corps of about eight hundred men was seen in the distance, marching here, the picket and outposts were withdrawn, and the regiment marched to McGowan's Pass where the Jaegers remained under arms, and thereafter marched to New York for embarkation.

Nothing was given over to the enemy. Also nothing was done to let him in, but an under-barracks-master was left on the barrier with the keys, which he was to deliver to the enemy commander, with the following letter:

Morris House, Nov. 21, 1783

Sir,
The present under-barracks-master has order to give you the keys to the defenses of the evacuated posts at Kingsbridge and McGowan's Pass.
I have the honor to be
 the most obedient servant
To: Major General L.J.A. de Wurmb
 Head Col.

Nov. 23 - General Washington with the governor and the members of the assembly of the government of New York had already arrived at Kingsbridge yesterday, and although New York should have been given over yesterday, this could not take place because too many things still had to be loaded, and General Carleton therefore postponed the evacuation until the 25th.

Everywhere in New York today, people have begun to show the American flags, which however, are being torn down, and this is causing various small disturbances. A commission was established to make arrangements to receive General Washington in triumph, with all pomp and ceremony.

Nov. 23 [sic] - As it was Sunday, everything was peaceful.

Nov. 24 - During the past night at about one o'clock, fire broke out in a brewery, resulting in several houses being burned down. This caused a general fear, as people for some time have feared the loyalists would set fire to the city. But this was only an accidental coincidence.

Nov. 25 - Today New York was finally abandoned. The general-in-chief and the admiral went aboard their ship, and the rest of the troops were brought to Staten Island in sloops, there to await their transports, which were expected hourly. Toward two o'clock in the afternoon, we raised anchor, and as the fleet sailed toward Staten Island, we saw the American flag being raised on several houses, but this did not occur at Fort George. By sunset, we had passed Sandy Hook, and as night fell, we lost sight of land.

Jaeger Corps Journal

Nov. 26 - The fleet consisted of fourteen sail. One ship was called *Mars*, with Colonel von Wurmb. Lieutenant Colonel von Prueschenck was on the *Sovereign*, and Major von Wurmb was on the *Peggy*. The weather was peaceful, no land was to be seen, and the wind was from the east. At noon we passed some transport ships which had come from England, in order to take on board the troops which were on Staten Island. During the night there was a moderate east wind.

Nov. 27 - The wind from the east blew fresh and it became stormy during the evening. Our mainsail tore, and at six o'clock it became necessary to take in all sail. It stormed exceptionally hard, with rain, and we were driven to the southward. The obvious danger of being thrown aground, in the vicinity of Cape Henry, passed about midnight, as the wind swung to the south, and toward morning to the west. The sea during the various winds became very high and rough. Most of the troops became seasick due to the motion of the ship, and we lost a cow and six sheep, which were drowned by the waves washing over the deck.

Nov. 28 - Brisk west wind. We sailed seven miles in an hour, and saw only three ships from the fleet. Our ship (the *Mars*) seemed to be a poor sailer, because it was too large and heavy, and unfortunately was under-manned, and among those on board, most were dull and lazy.

Jaeger Corps Journal

Nov. 29 - The wind remained westerly, very weak during the day, but stronger at night, otherwise dull weather.

Dec. 1 - The wind remained southwesterly. The skies cleared and the wind grew steadily stronger. At seven o'clock in the morning we lowered our sails, and while lowering the middle topmost sail, the man at the rudder was knocked down by a heavy crash [of a wave] and the ship swung around, the sail fluttered, and lay against the mast, which was in danger of crashing overboard at any moment. Nevertheless, the captain finally took the ship out of danger by cutting and lowering the sail. The wind remained southwesterly all day, and blew so strong that it drove us four miles without our using the least sail. At four o'clock the next morning, Dec. 2, the wind became westerly and more moderate, so that we set a small sail.

The sea was very high and we held our course of east by west [sic-probably should be east by north] with the wind. We saw a ship in the distance.

Dec. 3 - We saw a ship during the day which was probably the same one we saw yesterday. The wind was southwesterly and quite light.

Dec. 4 - Rain and squalls (buffeting by the wind) from the southwest. It cleared about noon and the wind became westerly, but easterly during the following night. No ships in sight.

Jaeger Corps Journal

Dec. 5 - Wind south by southwesterly with dull weather, course east by north. During the afternoon, a frightful southeasterly wind arose and we sailed onward at nine miles per hour.

Dec. 6 - Southwesterly wind with rain, becoming northwesterly. We sailed onward at nine miles per hour, and believed we were near the Banks of Newfoundland.

Dec. 7 - Northwesterly wind, cold and thick weather. We saw several ducks and believed we could find bottom. We dropped the lead to a depth of eighty fathoms, but to no avail.

Dec. 8 - Thick weather. Observation: 42° 47' north latitude with southwesterly wind.

Dec. 9 - Cold weather. We saw a ship and waited for it. It was the *Hope,* with part of the 80th Regiment on board. We steered toward them so that we could sail together.

Dec. 10 - Rainy and cold. North-northwesterly wind, which blew rather briskly. The *Hope* moved steadily southward.

Dec. 11 - Wind from the north-northwest, very strong. We saw nothing more of the *Hope*. Observation: 43° 45'. It became necessary for us to take in all sail, as it began to storm. In the night, we lost the figurehead from our ship, which exposed us to much danger. About midnight we set a sail.

Dec. 12 - Still stormy under a bright sky. We tried

to secure our mast, because we expected it would go overboard at any moment.

Because of the bad weather, however, there was not much that we could do. Observation: 43° 11'.

Dec. 13 - East wind all day, course south-southeast. We turned about three o'clock and sailed to the north. The wind changed more and more to the south. The weather was dull and mild.

Dec. 14 - Southeasterly wind, course east by north, rainy, unpleasant weather.

Dec. 15 The same. Observation: 46° 02'.

Dec. 16 - Dull and calm.

Dec. 17 - The same.

Dec. 18 - Calm, bright weather. Observation: 47° 12'.

Dec. 19 - Wind from the south, course east by south, bright weather, fresh wind. A ship in the distance.

Dec. 20 - Wind southwesterly, seven miles in an hour. Observation: 48° 12'.

Dec. 21 - Northwesterly [wind], six miles [per hour]. Observation: 48° 32'. Toward evening the wind became easterly. The night was serene.

Dec. 22 - Pleasant weather, light westerly breezes. Observation: 48° 48'.

Dec. 23 - Cloudy, little wind.

Dec. 24 - Northwesterly wind, toward one o'clock it began to blow very strongly.

Jaeger Corps Journal

Dec. 25 - The same strength, but a good wind. Observation: 49° 22'. We believed we would find bottom on the English coast next morning, if the wind would continue steady.

Dec. 26 - We threw the lead to no avail. The wind became easterly and stronger.

Dec. 27 - A strong east wind. We already were seeing some land birds, apparently blown from the land. Observation: 48° 44', and according to our reckoning, just off the entrance to the English Channel, which was at a distance of about six hundred miles.

Dec. 28 - East wind with squalls.

Dec. 29 - Wind southwesterly, stormy weather. We saw a ship and waited it. It was the *Dispatch* out of Oporto for Waterford, with wine. At twelve o'clock the wind became very strong, and a full storm toward evening. The night was one of the most dangerous and unpleasant. We still had two sails up, but could not lower them without certainly losing our mast, which was likewise in bad condition. From midnight until two o'clock during the night, the storm was most severe, and lasted until Dec. 30-- at four o'clock in the afternoon, when it finally began to rain, which caused the wind to abate somewhat. At five o'clock in the evening, it grew light in the west and the wind decreased noticeably. The sea, however, was exceptionally high so that we could spread no sails.

Jaeger Corps Journal

During the night, we caught a raven and a number of other birds, which the wind had blown from the land, and which had sought refuge on the ship.

Dec. 31 - Dull and dreary weather. The sea continued restless.

Jaeger Corps Journal

1784

Jan. 1 - Calm weather. We saw numerous land birds, which often fell into the water due to exhaustion, and drowned.

Jan. 2 - Finally, the wind began to blow from the northwest. We saw a ship from Lisbon bound for Ireland.

Jan. 3 - Westerly winds at seven miles per hour. The night was still.

Jan. 4 - Easterly winds. We found bottom at eighty fathoms. We saw four ships.

Jan. 5 - Easterly winds. We saw seven ships.

Jan. 6 - Wind from the south-southeast. The weather was as we would wish. At noon, we saw a ship from London, which told us it had left the Lizard this morning at nine o'clock, and that it lay just east by north, at a distance of eleven leagues. At that time we steered east by south, and had the wind by two points in our favor We saw land at two o'clock in the afternoon. During the night it was rainy and windy, and we nearly had to turn back out to sea, but fortunately, the wind turned.

Jan. 8 - Pleasant weather. By evening we were opposite Plymouth.

Jan. 9-13 - A continuous calm and warm weather, which prevented our journey from progressing, although we could see land, all the while at a distance of two miles.

Jaeger Corps Journal

Jan. 14 - The wind blew from the west. During the previous night we passed Portsmouth and arrived this evening at Dungeness. As it was too dark, we had to lay to. All night the wind was strong, and on the following morning we found ourselves near the French coast.

Jan. 15 - We passed Dover at one o'clock and dropped anchor at Deal, in the Downs, at two-thirty in the afternoon. The wind was very strong, and we could not approach land in order to send instructions.

Jan. 16 - We were ordered to return to Portsmouth, where the rest of the Jaegers were to be found. The ship's captain however, explained the situation of his ship, declaring it un-seaworthy. We were therefore to sail to Chatham. From today until the 26th, we had continuous northwesterly wind, which was so strong that no ship could sail, and we were therefore landed, despite the very many dangers. Some of our ships got loose from their anchors, and were seriously damaged. Also, we lost one ship, near Margate Road, at eight o'clock in the evening of the 22nd. However, we had no further misfortunes, and were able finally to sail up the Thames River, until Jan. 27--when we arrived at Sheerness, where we debarked and were given quarters, because there was no more room in Chatham. The barracks were very good, but the officers' quarters were bad.

Apr. 4 - The Hessian troops at Chatham and

Jaeger Corps Journal

Sheerness went aboard their transport ships, and sailed on Apr. 14--to Germany, where they arrived after a pleasant voyage on April 20, near Bremerhaven, and from which place they were transported aboard Weser boats on the Weser to Kassel.

May 17 - The Jaeger Corps arrived in Kassel, passed in review along with the Grenadier Battalion Linsinger, and a portion of the Donop Regiment, at His Serene Highness' riding school, and were then mustered during the afternoon

All native Hessians were given leave, and those non-Hessians no longer desiring to serve were given their release from service, as well as three months' pay. The entire Jaeger Corps however, was assigned, part in regiments, and those who wished to return to their profession as hunters, received half pay, until they could obtain employment as such..

Hesse-Cassel Jaeger Officers

"Das Feldjaeger-Corps von Hessen-Kassel Im Amerikanischen Unabhaegigkeitskrieg, 1776-1783"

"The Hessen-Cassel Field Jaeger Corps in the American War of Independence, 1776-1783"

A typed-script by Hans Konze, Sudenstrasse 8, 3578 Schwalmstadt 2 (Ziegenhain), Germany, 1982

Appendix II - Officers of the Hessen Field Jaeger Corps

Carl Emil von Donop - Colonel and aide-de-camp, Commander of the Grenadier and Jaeger Brigade. One of the most heroic and beloved officers. Died during the storming of Redbank in 1777.

Ludwig Johann Adolph von Wurmb - Lieutenant colonel, later colonel. After Donop's death, commander of the Jaeger Corps. One of the most distinguished leaders of light troops, who contributed greatly to the success and reputation of the Jaegers. 1806 - Lieutenant general and commander of Kassel. Died 1813.

Hesse-Cassel Jaeger Officers

Ernst Carl von Prueschenck - Major, then lieutenant colonel. Transferred from the Dragoons to the Jaeger Corps in 1771, with whom he was often cited for his courageous leadership. After the war he returned to the Cavalry, but he again returned to the Jaegers, in the Netherlands, in 1793. He was disqualified for further field service by a serious wound, and died in 1800 as a major general and commandant of Ziegenhain.

Philipp von Wurmb - Major, was transferred from the Infantry to the Jaegers in 1778, and back to the former after the war. In 1806, major general and proprietor of the von Wurmb Regiment. Died in 1808 in retirement.

Carl August von Wreden - Captain, commanded a company of field jaegers during the first two years with distinction, then took his release and served with the Darmstadt service, in which he was rapidly promoted to colonel, but died in 1791.

Johann Ewald - Captain, the real developer of the Jaeger Corps from a small beginning. He was primarily responsible for its training during the war and this largely contributed to his fame. His

Hesse-Cassel Jaeger Officers

exceptional talents and bravery in small unit combat enabled him in numerous situations to overcome larger combined units. Few officers in the British-Hessian Army had such a reputation, and occupied such an outstanding position of worth and trust, even from the commanding generals. In the year 1788, he received recognition in the Danish service with the rank of lieutenant colonel and command over a Holstein Jaeger Corps, to be organized by him. There too, he soon earned the general and highest respect, was raised to the nobility, received the Grand Cross of the Danebrogor Order, the rank of lieutenant general, and finally his position of commanding general of Holstein, and died in 1813.

Friedrich Heinrich Loray - Staff captain, then captain. The primary officer of the Jaeger Corps after the Seven Years' War, during which he rose from private in the mounted jaegers to officer. From the winter of 1776, he commanded the mounted jaegers in America, until a second wound in 1780 disqualified him from further service, and he returned to Europe, where he died of his wound.

Friedrich Wilhelm von Grothausen - First lieutenant, transferred from the Cavalry to the Jaegers in 1776. Commanded a half-company at Trenton, where

Hesse-Cassel Jaeger Officers

he did not conduct himself the best. In the counterattack against that place, he was wounded and killed.

<u>Ernst Friedrich Wilhelm von Donop</u> - First lieutenant, transferred from the Cavalry to the Jaegers in 1776, and died early in the spring of 1777, at New York.

<u>Johann Friedrich Jacob Trautwetter</u> - First lieutenant, then staff captain. Ewald called him "a marvel of bravery". During the Battle at Brandywine he was fatally wounded, and died soon thereafter.

<u>Georg Hermann Heppe</u> - Transferred from the Cavalry to the Jaegers as a staff captain in 1777, and on 25 September of the same year, he was shot and killed, near Glouchester in Delaware.

<u>Carl von Rau</u> - Initially a second lieutenant, later a captain. Assigned in 1777 to the mounted jaeger company. 1781, having already received a severe wound, he was in possession of orders to return to Hesse, when he led an assault on a guard post beyond Kingsbridge, and was shot and killed.

Hesse-Cassel Jaeger Officers

<u>Carl Moritz von Donop</u> - First lieutenant, then captain. Transferred from the Infantry to the Jaegers in 1777, and then back to the Infantry in 1784.

<u>Johann Heinrichs (Hinrichs)</u> - Lieutenant, then captain. Wounded several times, most severely during the capture of New York, at which time he received a ball in the chest. In 1784 he transferred to the Infantry, but soon took service with Prussia, where he was raised to the nobility, and promoted to lieutenant general. He died in 1834.

<u>Franz Christian von Bodungen</u> - First lieutenant, and then staff captain. He was only in America between 1777 and 1781, and then transferred to the Infantry, in Hesse.

<u>Friedrich Adolph Julius von Wangenheim</u> - First lieutenant, and then staff captain. Entered the Hessian Jaeger Corps from the Duke of Gotha's service in 1777, and remained therein, even after the war.

<u>J.W. von Hagen</u> - Lieutenant, then staff captain. Joined the Jaegers in 1777, and died at New York in 1782.

Hesse-Cassel Jaeger Officers

Erich Carl von Hagen - Lieutenant, and then staff Captain. Like his brother, he joined the Jaegers in 1777. On 25 November of the same year, he was dangerously wounded. After the war, he was assigned to the Infantry.

Friedrich Kellerhaus - Second, then first lieutenant and adjutant. Transferred from the Cavalry to the Jaegers in 1777, and back to the first in 1784.

Johann Heinrich Wolff - Second, and then first lieutenant. Assigned to the Jaegers in 1777, and transferred to the Engineer Corps in 1784.

DeMessy, Montluisant, and DeFasquiel - Three Frenchmen. The first two were taken into service as lieutenants in 1777. The third was transferred from the Guards to the Jaegers, as a first lieutenant in 1779. None of the three wished to fight against their countrymen who were united to the Americans. Only the first one remained in service, until he received his long requested release in 1781. The second apparently joined only to get free passage to America, where he immediately requested his release. He was captured trying to escape to the Americans, and sent as a prisoner to England. The third took leave soon after his transfer [to America ??] and was never seen again.

Hesse-Cassel Jaeger Officers

Johann Ernst von Wintzingerode - First lieutenant. Transferred from the Guards to the Jaegers in 1779, and back to the first in 1784. He then entered Prussian service, and retired as a captain.

Johann Schaeffer - Promoted to lieutenant from jaeger sergeant in May 1777. He remained in the Jaeger Corps until 1784. He entered Darmstadt service as a captain in 1790, eventually being promoted to lieutenant general and minister of war. Prior to that time, he had taken his family name of Schaeffer von Bernstein.

Alexander Wilhelm von Bickel - Sergeant [Oberjaeger], then second and first lieutenant. Remained with the Jaegers until he received a position of forester in 1788. The death, which often threatened him from enemy fire and on the ocean, awaited him in the ground. He fell into a pit in the Stahlberg Mountains near Schmalkalden, in 1810.

Maximilian Cornelius - Sergeant, then second lieutenant. Remained in the corps until 1784, then entered civil service and died in 1828, on pension as a senior treasurer on his estate at Breitenau.

Hesse-Cassel Jaeger Officers

Engelhard Boettiger - Transferred from the Dragoons to the Jaegers as a second lieutenant in 1779, and then back to the first, in 1784.

Johann Conrad Fliess - Second lieutenant. Joined the Jaegers in 1778. He also served in the Jaegers in the Netherland's War, where he received the rank of staff captain, and the Order Pour la Vertu Militaire. He died as a member of the nobility, and as colonel of the Crown Prince Regiment, in 1816.

Gotthilf von Gerrisheim (Griesheim) - Second lieutenant. Joined [the Jaegers] from Prussian service in 1780, and took his release in 1786.

Adam Ludwig Ochs - Sergeant, after 1781, second lieutenant and adjutant. Remained with the corps after the war, being promoted and raised to the nobility. 1806, lieutenant colonel. 1809, brigadier general in Spain, 1810, division general, and as such in Russia. Died in 1823, as Electoral Hessian major general.

Franz Georg Bauer - Sergeant, after 1782, second lieutenant. After the war he became the forester in Moerschen.

Hesse-Cassel Jaeger Officers

<u>Balthasar Merz</u> - Lieutenant, and then captain Transferred from the Cavalry to the von Buenau Regiment, and during the war performed duty with the mounted jaegers, performing many exceptional feats.

<u>Berthold Romstedt</u> - Staff captain, who remained behind in Kassel, doing recruiting duty in Waldau, until he returned to civilian status in 1781.

<u>W.L.K. von Eschwege</u> - Assumed Romstedt's duties in 1781, and at the same time was a master forester.

<u>Sir George Hangher</u> - Later Lord Coleraine. Chose to serve with the Jaeger Corps, which he joined in 1778, as a staff captain. In order not to impede the promotion of others, he removed himself from consideration. He also served in the military family of the British commander-in-chief. Subsequently, he became an Electoral Hessen major general on the ruler's staff, and died in 1840.

INDEX

ABERCROMBY, Col 146 170 Lt Col 94 Lt Col Robert 12
AGNEW, Gen James 23
ANDERSON, Maj 143
ANDRE, Maj John 130
ARBUTHNOT, Adm 127-128 139-140 144 150 Vice Adm Marriot 72
ARNOLD, Gen 132 135 140-141 146-147 150 162-163 Maj Gen Benedict 129-131
BARRAS, Paul Francois Jean Comte De 139 Mr De 150 162 164
BARRINGTON, Adm James 56
BAUER, Lt Franz Georg 178 201
BERNSTEIN, Schaeffer Von 200
BICKEL, Sgt Alexander Wilhelm Von 200
BICKELL, Lt Alexander Wilhelm 52 65
BLAND, Col 87
BODUNGEN, Capt Franz Christian Von 103 198
BOETTIGER, Lt Engelhard 201
BOUVILLE, Marquis De 172
BRANT, Joseph 66

BURGOYNE, Gen 28-29 Gen Sir John 25
BUTLER, Col John 49 66 Gen John 141
BYRON, Adm 71 77 Adm John 48
CAMPBELL, Brig Gen John 24 Col Archibald 57 Lt Gen 176 Lt Gen John 157 Maj 170
CARLETON, Gen Sir Guy 173 184 Sir Guy 174
CARLSON, R 13
CLINTON, Gen 28 45-46 50-51 61 80 85 121-122 130 134-135 139 161 173 Gen Sir Henry 25 Sir Henry 38-39 84 171
COCKBURN, Col 172
COLERAINE, Lord 202
COLLIER, Commodore George 70 Sir George 73
COLLINS, Capt 98
CORNELIS, Maximillian 41
CORNELIUS, Lt Maximilian 200
CORNEY, Lord 91
CORNWALLIS, Charles Lord 2 7 9 11 12 16-20 23 29 30 33 42 45 69 74-76 129 132

CORNWALLIS (cont.)
  136-137 141 145 149 157-
  158 162 165 168-171
CRAMMON, Capt 33
CRAMON, Capt Christoph
  August 1
CRILLON, Duc De 173
DALLING, Gen Sir John 74
DAYTON, Col Elias 123
DE GRASSE, Comte 150 162
  174
DEFASQUIEL, Lt 199
DELANCEY, Oliver 54
DEMESSY, Lt 199
D'ESTAING, Charles Hector
  Comte 48 50 71 79-80
  Monsieur 56
DIGBY, Adm Robert 165 175
DONOP, Capt Carl Moritz Von
  52 198 Col Carl Emil Kurt
  Von 25 Col Carl Emil Von
  194 Col Von 26 Lt Ernst
  Friedrich Wilhelm Von 197
DRAKE, Adm Francis Samuel
  167
DUBUY, Maj Johann
  Christian 86
DUNDAS, Col 146 Thomas 94
DYKE, Col 42
EBENAUER, Lt Friedrich 119
EMMERICH, Lt Col Andreas
  53 Lt Col 64 152-155
ERKSINE, Maj Gen Sir
  William 59-63
ESCHWEGE, W L K Von 202
EVANS, Capt 97

EWALD, Capt Johann 2 7 150
  195 197 Ewald Capt 7 12-
  13 38 52 89 96 101 103-
  104 110 126 143-144 157
  Ewald Gen 132
FERGUSON Maj, 108 110-111
  Maj 131
FLEURY, Col 68
FLIES, Lt 153
FLIESS, Lt Johann Conrad
  201
FOCKS, Capt 167
FORSTER, Lt 15
FULLER, Tom 90
GALVEZ, Don Bernardo 157
GATES, Gen Horatio 51 60 62
  129
GERRISHEIM (GRIESHEIM),
  Lt Gotthilf Von 201
GRANT, Maj Gen James 7 Maj
  Gen 9 11 16 54
GRAVES, Adm 125 140 160
  162 164 171
GRAY, Maj Gen Charles 17 50
  51
GREEN, Col Christopher 26
  Gen 30 Gen Nathanael 129
GREENE, Gen 136 141 148-
  149 160 172
GROTHAUSEN, Lt Friedrich
  Wilhelm Von 196
HACHENBERG, Maj Gen 116
HAGEN, Capt Erich Carl Von
  199 Capt J W Von 198
HAMMOND, Commodore 75
  Sir Snape 4 99

HAND, Brig Gen 66
HANGHER, Sir George (Lord Coleraine) 202
HEINRICHS (HINRICHS), Capt Johann 198
HEPPE, Capt Georg Hermann 197
HINRICH, 115
HINRICHS, Capt Johann 87 97 Capt 100-103 113 151 154
HOOD, Adm 150 161 172 Adm Sir Samuel 135
HOPE, Lt Col 113
HOTHAM, Commodore 160 Lt 27
HOVEDON, Richard 41
HOWARD, Col John 86
HOWE, Gen 3 8 15 17 21 25 28 32 34 38 Gen Robert 57 Gen Sir William 2 Lord 49 Lord Richard 48 Maj Gerald 77 Sir William 7 12 39
HUGER, Gen Isaac 142 143
IRVINE, Gen James 126
JOHANN, Ewald 1
JOHNSTON, Commodore 163 Lt Col Henry 64
KALB, Maj Gen Johann 129
KELLERHAUS, Adj Friedrich 199
KLING, Lt Jacob Ernst 103
KNYPHAUSEN, Lt Gen Wilhelm Freiherr 7 Gen Von 12 21 44-46 82 118

KNYPHAUSEN (cont.) Lt Gen Von 11 15 17 22 38 40 42 51 81 83 115 173
KONZE, Hans 194
KOSPOTH, Maj Gen Henrich Julius Von 59
LAFAYETTE, Maria Joseph Marquis De 38-39 138 147-148 158
LANGUARA, Adm Don Juan De 85
LEE, Gen Charles 47 Lt Col 142 Maj 71 Maj Henry 52
LESLIE, Maj Gen Alexander 40 89 131 Gen 93 113 132 136
LINCOLN, Gen Benjamin 66 69 78 80 85 Maj Gen 113
LINSINGEN, Lt Col 113
LOOS, Col Johann August Von 16
LORAY, Capt Friedrich Heinrich 196
LOREY, Capt 120 Friederich Henrich 25
LOSSBERG, Lt Gen Friedrich Wilhelm Freiherr Von 173 174 177 Maj Gen 116
LUDLOW, Col Gabriel 175
MAIDLAND, Col John 69 78-80
MATHEW, Brig Gen 59 Maj Gen 63
MATHEWS, Gen Edward 57 117 124 Maj Gen 116 123

MAXWELL, Brig Gen 66 Maj Gen 116 Maj Gen William 41
MCLAIN, Brig Gen 70 73
MEADOWS, Maj William 56
MERTZ, Lt Balthasar 13 Lt 36 52 84
MERZ, Capt Balthasar 202
METZNER, Capt 173
MOLO, Lt 97
MONCRIEF, Maj 97 Maj James 79
MONTCRIEF, Maj 94
MONTLUISANT, Lt 199
MORGAN, Daniel 42 Gen 136
MOULTRIE, Maj Gen 113
MUHLENBERG, Maj Gen Peter 143 146
MURRAY, Gen 173
MUSGRAVE, Brig Gen 176 Lt Col 44 Lt Col Thomas 22
NORTON, Col 84
OCHS, Sgt Later Maj Gen Adam Ludwig 201
PARKER, Adm Peter 77
PATTERSON, Gen 85 Maj Gen 89 106
PATTISON, Maj Gen James 59 60
PETTERSON, Gen 88
PHILIPPS, Maj Gen William 135 137-139 143 147-179
PHILLIPS, Gen 146
PIGOT, Adm Hugh 175-176 178
PIQUEST, La Mottres 160

POOR, Brig Gen Enoch 66
POTTER, Brig Gen James 66
PREVOST, Maj Gen Augustine 62 Gen 66 78-79 88
PRUESCHENCK, Lt Col Ernst Carl Von 7 195 Lt Col Von 124 126 152 156 185 Maj Ernst Carl Von 1 Maj Von 2 51 59
PULASKI, Count Casimir 80
RAU, Capt Carl Von 152 197 Capt Von 156
RAWDON, Francis Lord 57 Lord 148 149 160
ROBERTSON, Lt Gen James 148-149
ROCHAMBEAU, Jean Baptiste Donatien De Vimeur Comte 156 171
RODNEY, Adm Sir George 85-86 129 135 138 150 157 174
ROEDER, Capt Friedrich Wilhelm? Von 124 Capt 137 150 Capt Von 131
ROMSTEDT, Capt 202
ROSEN, Tom 93
RUTHERFORD, Maj Gen 129
SALTON, Capt 163
SCAMMEL, Col Alexander 155
SCHAEFFER, Lt Johann 153 200
SCHALLERN, Capt Henrich Sebastian Von 71
SCHEFFER, Lt Johannes? 103

Jaeger Corps Journal

SCOTT, Capt William 12 Gen Charles 51
SIMCOE, Col John Graves 146 Lt Col 157
SKINNER, Brig Gen 151
SMALLWOOD, Gen William 23
STEIN, Maj Johann Friedrich Georg Von 77
STEPHANS, Gen Edward 142-143
STERLING, Maj Gen Thomas 67-68
STEUBEN, Friedrich Wilhelm Von 147
STEWARD, Commodore 166 Maj 69
STIRLING, Gen 82 116 120-121
STIRM, Maj Gen Johann Daniel Von 46
STIRN, Gen 11
SULLIVAN, Gen John 50 Gen 78 Maj Gen 66
SUTHERLAND, Capt 95
TARLETON, Col Banastree 65 74 111 Lt Col 136
THOMAS, Col Evan 62
THOMSON, Lt Col 173 178-180
TOMKINS, Capt 89
TRAUTWETTER, Capt Johann Friedrich 15 Capt Johann Friedrich Jacob 197
TRAYTON, Tom 90
TRYON, Maj Gen William 65-67 116 123 126 Gov 72
VANDEREN, 21
VAUGHAN, Gen John 28 Gen 65 67 Maj Gen 59-60
VERNIER, Maj 88
WALDENFELS, Capt 131
WALLACE, Sir James 29
WANGENHEIM, Capt Friedrich A J Von 76 Capt Friedrich Adolph Julius Von 198 Capt Von 115 162
WANGHEIM, Capt Von 155
WARD, Capt Thomas 126
WASHINGTON, Gen George 12-13 16 19 21 31-32 34 39 45 47-48 53 62 68 78 80 82 109 119 125 128 130 136 138 141 156 161 165 171 182-184 Col William Augustine 142
WAYNE, Gen Anthony 18 Gen 68 145 Maj Gen 133
WEBSTER, Col 93-94 97 106 Lt Col James 64 68
WHITE, Col 79 Lt 74
WILLIAM HENRY, Prince, 86 165-166
WILLIAM IV, 86
WILLIAMS, 111 134 Capt 110 Gen Ortho A 131 Sgt 133
WILSON, Maj Gen Sir Thomas Spencer 29
WINTZINGERODE, Lt Johann Ernst Von 102-103 105 127 200
WOLFF, Lt Johann Heinrich 199

WOODFORD, Gen 98
WREDE, Carl August Von 1 2
  7-8 18-19 29-30
WREDEN, Capt Carl August
  Von 195
WURMB, Col Von 7 116-117
  176 177 180-182 185 Lt
  Col Ludwig Johann Adolf
  Von 1 Col L J A De 183 Lt
  Col Ludwig Johann Adolph
  Von 194

WURMB (cont.)
  Lt Col Von 2 8 14 21-22 37
  48 53 63-64 70 118 121-
  122 128 137 151-152 154-
  156 161-162 167 173-175
  Maj Gen Friedrich Wilhelm
  Von 177 Maj Philipp Von
  195 Maj Von 126 185 97
  Philipp Von 25

THE AUTHOR

Bruce E. Burgoyne was born 25 October 1924 in Benton Harbor, Michigan, and is married with three grown sons. His wife Marie, a Doctor of Education from the University of Southern California, is a helpful research companion and source of encouragement. Mr. Burgoyne's education includes a Master of Arts in Social Science (History, Economics, and Government) from Trinity University in San Antonio, Texas, plus course work at half a dozen other colleges and universities in America and overseas. He has also completed numerous military courses in such subjects as German language, Counterintelligence, and Public Information.

His employment, in addition to recently teaching a seminar course on the Hessians at Delaware State University, has included twenty years of military service in the Navy, Army, and Air Force, and six years as a civilian intelligence officer with the Army. During his military and civilian service he lived six years in Germany during which time he attended German language school in Oberammergau and two months of in-depth study, living in German households and undergoing Berlitz-type training. His daily duties required interviewing and interrogating in German, which further developed his knowledge of the language.

His forty years of research on the role of the Hessians in the American Revolutionary War have taken him and his wife to archives in England and Holland, as well as those in Germany and the United States, and resulted in the translation of more than 35 major Hessian documents.

www.ingramcontent.com/pod-product-compliance
Lightning Source LLC
Chambersburg PA
CBHW071441150426
43191CB00008B/1189